D0709492

WINE
BY
THE
GLASS

WINE
BY
THE
GLASS

OZ CLARKE

PAVILION

First published in the United Kingdom in 2018 by
Pavilion Books Company Limited
43 Great Ormond Street, London WC1N 3HZ

www.pavilionbooks.com
www.ozclarke.com

ISBN 978-1-91159-520-5   **33614080726580**

A CIP catalogue record for this book is available from the British
Library.

10 9 8 7 6 5 4 3 2 1

Reproduction by Mission Productions, Hong Kong
Printed and bound by 1010 Printing International Ltd, China

This book can be ordered direct
from the publisher at
www.pavilionbooks.com

For wine recommendations, special offers and news on Oz's
upcoming books and events visit www.ozclarke.com and sign up to
the Oz Clarke newsletter. Follow Oz on Twitter @OzClarke

HELLO

My name is Oz. Welcome to my
world of wine. This is a world
where wine is about pleasure, about
laughter, about friendship and fun,
but also about flavour, personality
and value. The world of wine
has never been more alive, more
energetic than it is now.

There has never been such an astonishing array of wines for us to choose from. Countries that I'd barely heard of 10 years ago are now clamouring for our attention. Grape varieties I feared had been consigned to the dustbin of history are glaring out at me from wine lists and merchants' shelves. And wine styles that I'd barely dreamt of, or perhaps I'd wistfully yearned for, are now commonplace, thrilling us all – if we're prepared to take the plunge.

Well, that's why I'm here. I've been taking plunges all my wine life. I admit, sometimes I've come up choking for breath, my throat burning with indignation at some of the concoctions I've confronted. But that's spurred me on to greater efforts and, between you and me, I don't mind bad wine now and then because it makes the myriad of good wines all about us seem all the more delicious.

But the wonderful thing about being a thirsty, enthusiastic wine drinker today is that there is very little genuinely bad wine around. In the good supermarkets and merchants, restaurants and bars, you can go right to the cheapest wine on offer, and still get pleasure from drinking the stuff.

Pleasure. Yes. That's what wine is all about for me. It's not about prestige or snobbery, it's not about marking out of 100 points and taxing my brain for the most unlikely descriptive adjectives. It's about the sparkle in my eyes and the joy in my heart.

But I do know that a bit of advice may not go amiss. So this is what I've tried to do here. I haven't written a book full of dry facts, statistics, pedestrian tasting notes and humdrum wine and food pairings. I've just tried to tell you about what I think will help you gain more pleasure from your wine. I've probably missed some things out, various aspects that other wine books religiously cover, but I simply didn't think they'd add to the sum of your pleasure.

There are plenty of details, quite a few facts and a whole ocean of opinions in this book. And if it makes you opinionated, but from the viewpoint of saying, I want more fun from my wine, I want to enjoy talking about it more with my friends, I want to pay a fair price, and I want to get the most flavour from my glass of red, white, pink or fizz – then I'll be happy. And I hope you will be too.

You can dip in and out of this book as much as you like – you don't have to read it from cover to cover, though I'd be delighted if you did. But let me just tell you what you've got coming up.

Basically, I'm trying to give a solid but not oppressive grounding, and then take you off into the rather fanciful and exotic world of my mind with its opinions. To start, I've chosen 12 words. Just 12. And I think if you understand these words you can have a pretty good wine life and never need to learn anything more.

But obviously I'd like you to. So I then take you to the grape varieties – the ones I think are attractive and important (that's not the same thing in some wine experts' eyes). Then I have a good old go at the various styles of wine you might encounter, or you might fancy. Then I talk about the concept of 'New World', because so many of the wines we like most come from there. And just to keep things lively I throw in some stuff about biodynamic, natural, organic and 'orange' wines; and what does terroir mean and how does a wine get oaky?

I haven't mentioned countries much yet, so I do a kind of speed date with all the wine countries of the world – well, almost all of them.

Then I talk about a whole load of practical stuff: what the label tells you, buying tips, is there such a thing as a bargain, how do you tell if you should age a wine, how do you tell if it's too old? Or too young? Oh, and lots of other things: essential kit, bottle shapes and glasses, food and wine matching, corkscrews and serving temperatures – it's all there.

Then I give you the chance to become a bit of a wine geek. I talk about wine tastings, blind and not blind, spitting (important), tasting terms, collecting, finding out more from the internet, wine societies and wine trips – and a lot of other stuff too.

And if you get through all of that, I hope you'll feel more confident in this world of wine, more able to make your own decisions, more able to approach the world of wine with a smile on your face and a sparkle in your eye.

START WITH THE BASICS

WINE AT A GLANCE

I sometimes think that you only
need to learn about 12 words to
have more wine knowledge than any
previous generation ever had. Just
12 words, plus six grape varieties
and six countries. And then you
will have enough basic knowledge
to enjoy wine pretty well for the
rest of your life. This is a bit of a
generalization, but here's how
it goes.

TWELVE WORDS OF WINE

To be honest, the best tasting note is often simply 'wow, that's good. Can I have another glass?' That's as good a tasting note as almost any wine will need. But sometimes you'll find yourself in situations where strange words start flying around. To make sure you can hold your own, here are 12 of the most common tasting terms.

1. Dry Well, let's start with the most basic term. Most reds, pinks and whites are dry. But what does dry mean? It means there is no sweetness in the wine. How come the word that means there isn't any liquid or fluid on a surface or in a substance ends up as the main descriptor for a glass of liquid – a glass of wine? I really don't know but once you get used to it, wines with no sugar, no sweetness, do seem to leave a drier (less liquid) sensation in your mouth. Or am I just being fanciful?

2. Sweet Sort of self-explanatory. Sweet wines have sugar sweetness in them. Everyone knows what I mean when I say a wine is sweet. In good quality wines, that sweetness will be from the actual juice of the grape itself (see page 62 for a bit more chat about how you make sweet wine). Only bargain basement stuff will have sacks of sugar thrown in to create sweetness.

3. Fruit You'll find some wine buffs getting awfully sniffy about the flavour of fruit in a wine. They should get out more. Loads of fruit doesn't have to mean that the wine tastes like a squirt of pineapple juice straight down your throat. But the grape is a fruit and, although you will hardly ever find a wine that tastes of the grape itself, fermentation transforms different grape varieties into wines that resemble all kinds of different fruits in their flavours. Some you'll find easy to pick up – green apples, lime, blackcurrant – but we'll all react differently because the wine is only *suggesting* these fruit flavours; there's nothing but grape juice in the wine. Fruit is fantastic. Revel in it.

4. Acid It may not sound nice, but acid is a fundamental part of the flavour of every fruit. A pineapple, a peach, an apple would taste dull as ditch water without acid. (Have you tried a French Golden Delicious recently?) The acid in fruit makes your mouth water and it transports perfumes and fruit flavour to your palate.

It's the same with wine. Acid in wine gives freshness, brightness and character to the taste. Without acid any wine tastes flat. You'll notice the acid more obviously in white wines like Sauvignon Blanc or Riesling, but acid also plays a big part in reds, even if it's less obvious. And acid also helps a wine to age well.

5. *Tannin* Tannin is that bitter, mouth-furring stuff that comes from the chewy grape skins or the grapes' pips and stems. When it isn't too dominant, i.e. if it doesn't suck all the moisture out of your cheeks, it gives an attractive chewy quality to the wine.

Tannin also stops a wine decaying, so a good tannin level will help a wine to age. But too much tannin is just unpleasant, so the most tannic wine is not necessarily the best wine on the table. The most balanced wine probably will be.

6. *Balance* How do you tell when a wine is balanced? It may sound strange, but usually you sort of know. It just feels better in your mouth, it tastes better and it leaves a better flavour when you've swallowed it. Balance refers to the relationship between acid (see above), tannin (ditto), fruit, alcohol and, if they have used barrels to make the wine, oakiness. Too much alcohol makes a wine taste and feel hot in your throat. Too much oak smothers a wine with creamy, spicy richness, too much tannin is bitter, too much acid is raw, and too much fruit...? Well, a wine *can* have so much fruit that it's just too much of a good thing, but in general, lots of fruit is a pretty attractive flavour. If these five components all seem to blend into a really nice experience when you put the wine in your mouth – that's balance. And balance helps a wine age, too.

7. *Bouquet* Well, technically this term means the smell of a wine that's getting quite mature. But, honestly, if you want to use the term – especially if a wine smells to you a bit like a bouquet of flowers – and quite a few wines do, praise be – then use it. You could say 'perfume' or 'aroma' or just simply 'smell', but if the mood takes you and the smell is a bit uplifting – say 'bouquet'. Why not?

8. *Length/Finish* When you hear wine buffs talking about 'length' they're simply discussing a wine's aftertaste. Good wines always have a fantastic lingering flavour – the aftertaste – that seems to well up in your throat after you've swallowed. Some old-timers call it the 'peacock's tail', i.e. how the taste spreads out in your mouth. One or two American wine critics even mark wines according to how many seconds the aftertaste lasts for. They must be gripping conversationalists. But it is worth just reflecting for a moment when you've swallowed a good wine because there's one last hurrah to come – the aftertaste, the finish, the length. Don't miss it.

9. Oxidized You'll hear this word now and then. Usually it means that a wine has got too old and is starting to taste dreary and flat and lifeless. A white wine may have gone a rather dark hue of gold. A red wine may have started to exhibit too much brown and not enough purple or blood red. But sometimes even a young wine tastes oxidized. So what does oxidized mean? It means that too much oxygen has got into the wine. Oxygen in small amounts helps a wine develop perfume and intriguing flavours. You can test this out by pouring out a glass of wine, tasting it, then leaving it for half an hour. All but the most crummy wines will have changed with exposure to the air. A young wine will improve. But an old wine might fade away. And there's the crux of the matter. Careful exposure to oxygen allows a wine to develop, but eventually the wine plateaus, then declines, and oxygen hastens this decline. Too much exposure to oxygen, even when a wine is still in the vat, destroys freshness and leaves a staleness, a tiredness right from the start, that never goes away.

10. Oaky You'll often hear people saying a wine is 'oaky'. This means that the basic wine flavour which comes from the grapes and their fermentation has been affected by aging a wine in wooden barrels – usually made of oak. Oak contains vanillin – creamy-scented, spicy, nutty. When you make a barrel, you heat staves of wood to bend them into the barrel shape. This heating is called 'toasting' and creates more flavours on the surface of the vanillin-laden wood – chocolate, fudge, nuts, toasted bread crust. So when you ferment a wine, or age it, in such a barrel, the liquid will absorb these flavours. If the winemaker doesn't want them in the wine, he'll use an older barrel because most of the oaky flavours will have already been dissolved into a wine the first time the barrel was used. Or he'll choose to make his wine in stainless steel tanks. These don't add any flavours at all and most fresh white wines are made in stainless steel.

11. Spicy There's actually a grape called Spicy Traminer –
Gewürztraminer. It's a German grape and it's certainly capable
of producing lush, heady wines dripping with boudoir scent. But
spice? Spice is usually thought of as a kitchen commodity – things
like cinnamon, ginger, nutmeg or cloves. You will occasionally smell
wines that have a real whiff of the kitchen spice cupboard, but the
word is more likely to be applied to wines that have rich fruit or floral
scents. Red wines that are rather succulent and lush and indulgent as
against dry and austere can be described as 'spicy' too. Some wines
share an exotic 'Middle Eastern kasbah' perfume, and they would be
dubbed 'spicy'.

12. Herbaceous and Vegetal These are two terms that can describe
very attractive flavours, but are generally employed as a negative
criticism. That's a pity. Herbaceous is normally a description of
any kind of 'green' flavours in a wine. Green flavours, especially
in a red wine, may show that the grapes weren't ripe at harvest,
but a seasoning of 'green' freshness is a hallmark of many of the
greatest red wines of France. In white wines, the crisp, zesty flavour
of springtime hedgerows or orchards and the nose-wrinkling
intensity of citrus fruit zest are often irresistibly refreshing in their
'herbaceous' way, and attempts to make the wine taste riper often
spoil the whole effect. 'Green' is often the colour of nature at its
freshest and most alluring. That can apply to wine flavours, too.

Vegetal is more likely to apply to a slightly grubby, muddy, 'carrots
or potatoes left to rot in the earth' kind of flavour. Not that nice.
But mature reds often develop a fascinating damp autumn leaf or
undergrowth character that is absolutely spot on and thoroughly
enjoyable. I think it's a sign that very few of us now drink mature reds
that such flavours can be easily misunderstood.

SIX GRAPE VARIETIES

I'm going to choose three red and three white varieties, for
simplicity's sake. The reds are Cabernet Sauvignon, Shiraz and Pinot
Noir. Merlot could be in there as a softer version of Cabernet and
it's often blended with Cabernet for this purpose. The whites are
Chardonnay, Sauvignon Blanc and Riesling. Riesling isn't as popular
as Pinot Grigio, but it is a more characterful grape.

THREE RED GRAPES

Cabernet Sauvignon This is grown in just about every country in the world where the sun shines plentifully. The wine is usually quite dark in colour, rather chewy in style but with good, black fruit flavours, and the more expensive examples will have rich, spicy, oak barrel tastes, too.

Syrah/Shiraz Shiraz wines are generally rich, lushly fruity and full of flavours like blackberry and chocolate and kitchen spice, whereas wines labelled as Syrah are usually drier and less rich.

Pinot Noir This is the palest of all the main red grape varieties, the gentlest, the most delicate. If you like gum-bashing reds, don't go for Pinot Noir, because Pinot is positively reserved in personality, low in bitterness (that's good) and smooth in texture. Although Pinot Noir is light it goes remarkably well with spicy food. Burgundy in France makes the most famous Pinot Noir wines (though you never see the grape name on the label there) and cooler parts of California, South Africa, Chile, Australia and New Zealand grow it well, too.

THREE WHITE GRAPES

Chardonnay A soft, golden style of wine, usually mellow and often made spicier and fuller by aging in oak barrels. Sometimes the wine can be appley, sometimes oatmealy and sometimes more tropical and peachy in flavour.

Sauvignon Blanc A sharp, green, crunchy style of wine, usually quite crisp, with a refreshing acid nip that makes your mouth water (in a pleasant way). The wine is not normally aged in oak barrels. So, if you're a member of the IHO (I Hate Oak) brigade, Sauvignon Blanc is usually a good bet.

Riesling Wine buffs often say Riesling is the finest white grape in the world, but regular wine drinkers rarely agree with them. They say they don't know whether Riesling wine is sweet or dry (it can be either, and everything in between), they don't know how to pronounce it – is it Ryezling? (no) or Reesling? (yes). And in a time when things German are not considered cool (except in Germany) people presume Riesling is German, therefore un-cool. Well, the grape is German but it's grown all over the world. The wine can be seriously dry with a slatey citrus acidity, off-dry with more fruit but still excellent acidity or really *very* sweet but still with tingling acidity. So it's very versatile, but confusing too. Tingly acidity and absolutely no new oak barrel-aging are two of its strongest points.

SIX COUNTRIES

In the modern world of wine, there are a lot more than six countries making waves. But we're talking about useful generalizations here, so I'll stick with six, three from Europe – France, Italy and Spain – and three from the New World – Australia, Chile and New Zealand.

France France makes every type of wine – red, pink and white, sweet, medium and dry, fizzy, still, light and fresh, powerful and oaky... find me a style and France will probably make it. But the most useful generalization is that the red wines are usually dry, often a bit short of obvious fruit, keeping some evident acidity and always with a little of that tannin chewiness. The whites are generally very dry – even the oaked wines are very dry to go with their oaky spice – and they usually have noticeable acidity. They are rarely a big mouthful of ripe, soft fruit. You can drink them by themselves, but they're probably better with food.

Italy People who love Italian wines usually also love – and I mean love – Italy, its lifestyle, its culture, everything Italian. And they chorus their love of Italian wines – especially reds – above all others. But Italian wines are much more difficult to learn about, appreciate and enjoy than those of most other countries, and they *really* are better with food – preferably Italian. The reds in general have more tannic bitterness, more acidity, more dark, impenetrable personality than most other reds. Whites can be surprisingly bright, scented and refreshing – but not in a green fruit, acid way. And most of them are not aged in oak. And what food goes best with Italian reds? Come on, you're not really asking that question...

Spain Spain is best known for red Rioja, sparkling Cava and fortified sherry. Three very distinct styles. Cava is a very good, dry fizz. Sherry is a thrilling type of wine, usually very dry but with an amazing array of flavours. Red Rioja is known for its soft, creamy style, but modern Rioja is often deeper and more rough-edged though still oaky. In general, Spanish reds are quite dark and oaky and have less bright personality than equivalent French examples. Spanish whites can be oaky, but nowadays are usually pretty lean and fresh – and often scented – not bad for a country as hot as Spain.

Australia Big, brawny, breezy, self-confident, sunny Australia. Well, it was by offering 'sunshine in a bottle' that Australia became famous for its wine. Many Aussie wines are more toned down today, but sunny, ripe flavours, easy to drink, easy to like, are what Australia still does better than anyone. If you like sun-ripened flavours with a smile on their face, Australia is the place for you.

Chile Chile started out more slowly as a wine-producing country than Australia, but it has, if anything, even more sunshine than Australia, along with disease-free vineyards and a host of cooling breezes to temper the sun. The reds are lush, rich, but not baked, full of dark, ripe fruit, but not jammy – real tasty mouthfuls with very little tannin to nip your gums. The whites have loads of fruit flavour, lovely freshness and extreme drinkability.

New Zealand The coolest (in temperature terms) of the New World tyros, but there is still lots of sun. This is New Zealand's genius. There are numerous spots on the North and South Islands where vines grow really well. White grape varieties will ripen everywhere and are led by snappy Sauvignon Blanc, but Kiwi Chardonnay is also bursting with fruit and personality. The red wines are mostly lighter and drier since the grapes struggle to ripen sometimes, and are led by gentle, tasty Pinot Noir. If you like freshness and crisp, uplifting flavours in your wine, head down New Zealand way.

GOOD GRAPE GUIDE

The grape variety is the most
important influence on how a wine
tastes. All grape varieties have
different flavours, giving different-
tasting wines. It's the same with
pears or plums or apples. A Golden
Delicious, a Granny Smith and
a Cox's Orange Pippin all taste
different. So do a Chardonnay, a
Sauvignon Blanc and a Pinot Grigio.

Learning which grape varieties you enjoy drinking – and which ones you don't – is one of your most important steps towards always choosing a wine you like.

So I've picked a top 10 of red and a top 10 of white varieties – the ones you're most likely to come across. If some of the top 10 are unfamiliar, that's OK. Just think, do they sound attractive? If they do, give them a try. If you're not sure, well, when did a glass of unfamiliar wine hurt anybody?

TOP RED GRAPES

Cabernet Sauvignon This is the big one. The biggest. The most widely planted. King Cab. It gets everywhere, it shoves aside the local grapes and muscles itself into the spotlight. Why? Well, first, all over the world it makes wine that tastes like Cab – dark, sometimes a bit tough, but with a big, dry taste of blackcurrants and plums and an appetizing streak of earthiness that gives you what you paid for just about wherever on the globe you find yourself.

Why did Cabernet Sauvignon become so successful? (By the way, you can just call it Cab or Cabernet if you want.) Because it's pretty easy to grow in most places, so long as there's a fair amount of sun. With global warming, more suitable places pop up every few years. And people liked making wine from it because the most famous red wine in the world is Bordeaux from south-west France. Cabernet Sauvignon is the most important Bordeaux grape (even though Merlot now accounts for over 50% of the plantings there). So if you planted Cabernet and called your wine Cabernet, whether you were in California or Canada, Argentina or Australia, Chile or China, you could bask in a tiny reflection of glory from Bordeaux's fame, as well as making a wine with a recognizable taste.

Syrah/Shiraz This is the spicy one. The one with rich, ripe, dark fruit flavours. It can be juicy, it can be jammy, it can be smoky or stewy or glinting with the cold, pure, rocky scent of granite and flint. It can be peppery and perfumed like lily sap or it can be judderingly powerful and thick as soup.

Pretty much everything, really, which explains why winemakers like it so much. It'll make a good stab at anything from pale pink to heady, sweet, fortified reds. It will grow in quite cool places so long as the sun shines – Switzerland can make good reds from it – as well as in some of the hottest vineyard spots in the world.

Syrah or Shiraz? Well, it's a French grape and the French call it Syrah. Around the world when people began to plant it, if they wanted to make a drier, less showy style of wine, i.e. like the French, they called it Syrah. But it was the Australians who made the grape famous with rich, beefy reds. And they called it Shiraz. Same grape, different name. So if someone in, Argentina, or South Africa, or Sicily, or even France, Spain or Portugal sometimes, wanted to make a rich, exotic style of wine, they called it Shiraz.

By the way, Shiraz is the name of the great winemaking city of ancient Persia. Could the Shiraz grape come from there? The scientists say 'no', but what do they know? I like to think it could be the original red wine grape to migrate from Asia to Europe. And when I think that, the wine tastes more exciting.

Pinot Noir The pale one. The delicate one. The scented one. The 'wine buff's' delight. It's supposedly just about the most difficult grape variety to grow properly in the whole world. It doesn't like too much heat because warm conditions turn its fresh personality into dullards' jam. It doesn't like getting rained on because it has some of the thinnest skin of any red wine variety and the grapes rot on the vine. It makes its historically great red wines in a tiny sliver of eastern France called Burgundy where the whole vineyard area is sometimes only a few hundred yards wide. And even there, most of the wines are not very exciting.

In fact, they call Pinot Noir 'the Holy Grail' for winemakers – both in Burgundy and all over the world. Isn't 'the Holy Grail' something you always search for but never find? That doesn't stop them trying in every corner of the globe. The trouble is if the textbook 'Burgundy' wine you're trying to copy is pale, delicate and subtly scented, it's a lot more difficult to copy than, say, Merlot where the textbook wine is succulent and rich.

Most New World countries plant their vines where there's loads of guaranteed sunshine – and it's almost always too hot for Pinot Noir. So in Australia, Chile, South Africa, Argentina and New Zealand they search for cooler, more marginal, more difficult spots to grow Pinot – places where they said it was too cold for vines to grow. Sometimes it works brilliantly. Sometimes it doesn't. In Europe the coldest parts of the winelands eagerly pursue Pinot. And since it makes fabulous sparkling wine in Champagne, sparkling winemakers in really cool conditions worldwide can use it for excellent fizz where it doesn't ripen well enough to make red wine.

Merlot The lush one. The sexy one. The succulent, juicy, easy-going one. And Merlot *is* easy to like, easy to understand and luckily it's also easy to grow, easy to make into wine – and easy to pronounce. In fact, Merlot's simple short name is one of the reasons it has been, at times, the world's favourite red wine grape. It's pronounced Merlow. Simple. A glass of Merlot. A lot easier to ask for than a glass of Cabernet Sauvignon. Two syllables versus six.

Merlot (like Cabernet Sauvignon) also hails from Bordeaux in south-west France, and it is used in blends to soften the tougher, darker Cab, as well as making soft, spicy wines largely on its own in St-Émilion and Pomerol on Bordeaux's Right Bank. It was these fruit-bombs that alerted the world to Merlot's crowd-pleasing qualities, and it spread like wildfire across Europe and the New World, making carefree glasses of wine wherever it set up camp.

But there's also a more serious side to Merlot. It *can* make some pretty profound wines in Bordeaux, impressive wines whose softness means they are ready to drink much more quickly than the powerhouse Cabernet Sauvignons. Other parts of Europe make big, serious but spicy Merlots. And the New World, in particular California, Chile and New Zealand, use Merlot to make some of their best reds.

Tempranillo You may not have seen this name on the label, but if you've drunk any red Rioja, you'll have drunk Tempranillo because it's the main Rioja grape. In fact, it's the main red grape in most of northern Spain – wines like Ribera del Duero and Toro are Tempranillo too – as well as appearing all over the centre and the south. It shouldn't really be grown so widely in Spain because it's an early-ripening grape, best suited to reasonably cool conditions. It ripens very quickly to high alcohol levels in warmer regions. Even so, Tempranillo is highly successful because its wine is juicy, not too deep or tough, full of ripe strawberry and black fruit, and it is well suited to being aged in oak barrels, which adds a spicy richness to the wine. It's also very important in northern Portugal, where it is usually called Roriz. Argentina has quite a lot of it, and we should see some interesting spicy examples soon. Australia, too, has some pretty good examples.

Sangiovese If you've ever had a glass of Chianti, you'll have been drinking Sangiovese wine. And if you've ever thought, hmm, what's causing that slightly sweet-sour taste, that slightly furry-edged chewiness, those dried herbs, that dried tomato skin flavour – well, that's the Sangiovese grape too.

Sangiovese is the main grape in Chianti, and in fact it's the most widely planted grape in several parts of Italy, from the centre to the south. But it rarely gives luscious, bright, fruity flavours. There's always something chewy, sometimes stewy, frequently acid-streaked about the wine. So it doesn't make brilliant wine for casual drinking by itself. But that slightly chewy, sweet-sour, herby style means it goes brilliantly with a wide array of Italian food. And in Italy, red wine's job is to go with the local food.

Efforts are being made to give it a chance in California, Australia and Mexico; the best results will probably come from Argentina.

Garnacha/Grenache This is a gorgeous, gut-filling beast of a grape – rich, sumptuous, often groaning with alcohol and the positively stewed dense fruit of a grape that simply loves to lounge about in the midday sun. Garnacha does need the heat, but repays its roasting with wines that are packed full of raisin, date and prune fruit, often brightened up by the scent of dried herbs.

The variety is Spanish, but its best known role is in France (where it's called Grenache) as the backbone of Châteauneuf-du-Pape from the Rhône Valley, one of France's most famous wines. It's the dominant variety in blends all over southern France. In Spain, it is a part of Rioja's blend but is at its best in Priorat near Barcelona, and a variety of regions in Navarra, Aragon and Castilla La Mancha. Mostly red, Garnacha rosé is a delight. Australia's Barossa has some very old Grenache vines.

Barbera This is one of those grapes that should be much better known. Its heartland is in Piedmont, in north-west Italy, where it manages to make rich, rather raisiny, plummy wines with refreshing acidity and low bitterness in a landscape where tannic bitterness in reds seem to be prized. Lombardy, next to Piedmont, also makes good use of it, as does Emilia-Romagna – it goes very well with Bolognese food, and continues to be grown further south, largely because it resolutely retains its fresh acidity even when the sun gets seriously hot. Barbera should be one of the most successful European grapes in the warm New World, but it has always simply been used as a cheap blender. California grows quite a bit, but Argentina and Australia give Barbera a bit more respect.

Cabernet Franc You won't often see this name on the label because most of the time Cabernet Franc is a junior blending partner in Bordeaux reds or in Cabernet Sauvignon and Merlot blends from elsewhere. But producers are at last realizing that Cabernet Franc is a smashing variety in its own right. The wines often have a mouth-watering raspberry fruit, a slightly chewy, green stem taste, and a suggestion of pebbles and stones. If that all sounds a bit strange, the France's Loire reds are usually from Cabernet Franc, and are some of the most refreshing in the whole country. Elsewhere in Europe, northern Italy grows quite a bit. Otherwise, it's beginning to shine in places like Canada, Brazil, Uruguay and Virginia in the USA.

Malbec If you said Malbec was an Argentinian grape variety, I wouldn't blame you because there's been a flood of Argentinian Malbec – juicy, rich, ripe, ever so easy to glug. Malbec has certainly found fantastic conditions to grow in the lee of the Andes mountains. But the grape actually comes from south-west France. It used to be quite important in Bordeaux but is a pretty minor player now. Its heartland is in Cahors, up the Dordogne Valley. Since Malbec gives extremely dark wine, I can see why it used to be called 'the Black Wine' of Cahors. Cahors is pretty dense and tough, tasting of tobacco and damson skins. You'll also find Malbec in Australia, New Zealand and Chile, but it's clearly happiest in Argentina.

Some tasty also-rans
Carignan Once jeered at as possibly the world's worst red grape, but old vines in France, Spain, Italy and Chile produce bright, rocky reds that are lapping up the love.
Carmenère A Chilean bobby-dazzler, originally misnamed Merlot, that gives dense, spicy, blackcurranty reds. Actually an old Bordeaux grape. Italy and China have some.
Cinsaut Pretty much dismissed as a pallid rosé replicant in southern France, it makes pale but palate-clicking, chewy, strawberryish reds in South Africa.
Corvina Just about the most joyous, juicy, jovial Italian grape you've never heard of. It's the core of the glugger's delight – Valpolicella – but it's also the sweet heart of powerhouse Amarone.
Dolcetto An Italian grape, whose name means 'little sweet one'. Hmm. Little chewy gum-stringer more often. But good Piedmont examples are purple-pink, lively and lovely. The New World is thinking it might be worth a punt.
Gamay We may not know the grape name, but most of us know the wine name – Beaujolais. France's happy juice is made from Gamay. Sappy, cherryish, stony – it's a glugger's delight, but can make dark serious wine, too.

Mourvèdre Mostly a tough old brute, making surly southern French reds tasting like pheasant hung a day too long. But it adds a lip-smacking savoury streak to Châteauneuf-du-Pape, and produces rib-sticking midwinter reds in Spain (as Monastrell) and Australia.

Nebbiolo Don't judge a book by its cover. This pale, dilute-looking red looks about as harmless as a church mouse, but it's the grape of Barolo in north-west Italy, whose wild strawberry and herb flavours are dense and grand – they need to be to stand up to the thwack of Nebbiolo's bitter tannins.

Pinotage The grape that doesn't do what it says on the tin. Created in South Africa in 1925, it was supposed to taste like Burgundy but it never did. At its best it tastes of mulberries and marshmallows toasted on a November bonfire. At its worst …

Primitivo The leading black grape in Puglia, southern Italy, producing rich, alcoholic wines. It has been enjoying a renaissance since being discovered to be the same as California's Zinfandel.

Tannat Uruguay's claim to fame. In fact, Tannat comes from south-west France, where it makes Madiran reds of Darth Vader density and malevolence. Uruguay's examples are still chewy and deep but sometimes almost disarming and scented.

Touriga Nacional This could be the best red grape you've never heard of. It's the beating heart of rich, sweet port from the Douro Valley, but is now making proud, assertive yet scented, dry red wines from the Douro and elsewhere in Portugal.

Zinfandel The Californians say it's the American First Grape, but in fact it comes from Croatia where they call it Crljenak Kaštelanski – yup, I'd change the name, too. Zin makes lots of soft, sweetish pink, but is at its best with big, chewy, self-confident, brambly, unsubtle, gob-stopping reds.

TOP WHITE GRAPES

Chardonnay Chardonnay is a village in Australia. Isn't it? Well, no, it's not. Actually, it's a village in France in the Burgundy region, which is where Chardonnay reigns supreme as their white wine grape. Many of the world's greatest whites are Burgundies from the Chardonnay grape. But Chardonnay became so linked in

---

Red wines have hundreds of different flavours, according to grape varieties, climate, soil and winemaking. Here are a few – chocolate, blackcurrant, plum, cherry and blackberry. White wine flavours can be fresh, lush or savoury. Here are a few – peach, apple, gooseberry, hazelnut and soft white bread.

everyone's mind with New World whites – all golden and soft and bursting out with peach and pineapple flavours and spicy, caramelly richness – that people forgot it was a grape. They really did think it was a village in Australia.

In fact, Chardonnay's real claim to fame is that for anyone under the age of about 50 it was probably the most important grape variety in the world because it ushered in the era of New World wines dominating our drinking. Ripe, soft, easy to like and easy to understand, Chardonnay became the poster girl for varietal wines, wines that labelled themselves according to their grape variety rather than by where they came from.

Didn't wines always do this? No, they didn't, and it wasn't until the Americans and Australians asked 'how do we simplify this wine labelling lark and try to tell our customers what the wine might taste like?' that people started putting the name of the grape variety on the front label. Since each grape variety is different and exerts the single biggest influence on the flavour of the wine, you'd have thought this was pretty obvious. Until the 1990s obviousness was the last thing the wine world seemed to be interested in. Then along came Chardonnay.

Chardonnay goes in and out of fashion, but it's a smashing grape. It'll grow just about anywhere, from Denmark in the north to Patagonia in the south, and is at its best in Burgundy in eastern France. It doesn't need that much heat, but it can still produce an OK drink when you grow it in the desert.

It's not that spicy or perfumed or fruity – sometimes it's actually rather neutral in a pleasant enough way. But it has a natural affinity with being fermented and aged in oak barrels – that's where you'll get your extra spice and perfume. And if you're struggling to ripen it, don't worry, it makes excellent fizz; Chardonnay is massively important in the best Champagnes.

Sauvignon Blanc The green one. The grassy one. The zesty, citrus, lip-smacking, mouthwatering, thirst-quenching one. That's Sauvignon – or Savvy as the New Worlders like to call it. It's a love it or hate it grape. A lot of wine buffs say they hate it. Why? Too much flavour? Too refreshing? Too easy to understand? Yup, all those things.

It's not often in the world of wine that a wine can be at its best when it's at its simplest. But when you try to complicate Sauvignon Blanc, try to make it more complex and intellectually challenging, you don't necessarily make a better wine. More expensive – yes. More likely to please the wine buffs – yes. But a better drink – no. That's the thing with Sauvignon Blanc. The wine buffs are never going to like it. Which is fine by me, so long as they don't keep persuading the winemakers to try to change it. Leave it alone. It's our grape. It's the wine drinkers' grape. And its sheer, upfront, obvious, in-your-face flavour is what makes it such a success.

Sauvignon makes green, sharp wine. So you do need fairly cool conditions, but you also need sun. So it grows brilliantly where there's lots of sun but unusually cool weather. South Island New Zealand works and areas of South and North America and South Africa chilled by Arctic or Antarctic Ocean currents are good too. And in Europe, cool south-west and western France does it best.

Riesling Riesling is a slightly divisive grape variety. Some wine people dote on it, some wine people don't get it at all. A small bunch of 'true believers' think Riesling is the finest grape on the planet. Well, I wouldn't go that far, but it does deserve some serious thought.

It's a German variety – which was great, until German wines fell out of fashion at the end of the 20th century and most of Eastern Europe used to call wine Riesling when it hadn't any Riesling grapes in it at all. And people could never work out if the wine was sweet or dry.

Well, it can be as dry as any wine in the world, and as sweet as any – and everything in between. But, unless the wine is German, where some of the best wines are delicate and scented and slightly sweet, most good Rieslings will be dry to very dry with a strong tingling acidity. Just a small number are made intentionally sweet – they'll say so on the label, and they'll be *very* pricey. Germany and Austria are still the best European producers, while Australian Riesling is some of the driest wine in the whole country (Clare Valley in South Australia makes some of the best). The USA makes Riesling in various places with New York State (especially the Finger Lakes) and Washington State being the most successful.

Muscat This is the variety that actually makes wine that tastes like the grape itself. Muscat is a delicious eating grape, full of sweet fruit and musky scent. And for once, the fermentation process doesn't transform the flavour too much – that gorgeous, heady, hothouse scented fruit comes through in the wine.

There are various sorts of Muscat – the best is called 'small berry' Muscat – and these grow all round the Mediterranean and as far north as Germany, making all kinds of wines, from bone dry to lush and sweet. The New World grows a fair amount, and in Rutherglen in Victoria, Australia, a brown version of the 'small berry' Muscat makes some of the richest, sweetest wine in the world.

Pinot Gris/Pinot Grigio I'm not sure Pinot Gris by itself would quite get into the top 10, but the Italian version of Pinot Gris – Pinot Grigio – has become such a worldwide favourite that I can't exactly leave it out. Yet it's become fantastically popular because it barely tastes of anything, yet manages to wear a bit of Italian 'chic' around its neck to make it irresistible. These Pinot Grigios are mostly from northern Italy and are cheap, though north-east Italy can take the grape more seriously. Pinot Gris (the French spelling but the same grape) makes really full-bodied, honeyed wines in Alsace, in eastern France. Germany, Austria and Hungary also do it well. You'll find it in the New World too, but only New Zealand has much success with Pinot Gris, making fruity, banana- and peach-scented whites.

Chenin Blanc Chenin Blanc comes from the Loire Valley in western France, where it makes all types of wine, from bone-dry to remarkably sweet. It's also a dab hand at fizz in places like Saumur and Vouvray. It's pretty high in acid and is difficult to ripen. Since fizz makers like high-acid grapes, they rub their hands during a cold vintage, but the other winemakers know they've got a struggle on their hands to deal with the acid and make charming wines. High acid is one of the reasons it is very popular in South Africa. The climate is hot, but Chenin can hold on to its acidity, meaning its wines can be bright and fresh or nutty and deep according to what the winemaker wants to do.

Albariño There has been such a surge of quality in Spanish white winemaking in the last decade, it now merits a place in the top ten. Albariño is the main white grape in Rías Baixas, which is the best white wine region in the rainy, breezy, but sunny north-west tip of Spain, Galicia. It makes one of the great seafood wines – zesty, lemony and humming with life. And that's a good thing, because Galician seafood is some of Europe's best. Northern Portugal also grows it (as Alvarinho) as part of the Vinho Verde blend – another ace seafood wine. California and New Zealand have picked up on Albariño. So did Australia till they discovered that what they were planting as Albariño was the entirely different Savagnin from the Jura in eastern France.

Gewürztraminer Love it or loathe it. This is a wonderfully divisive grape with lots of wine geeks complaining that the wine is too perfumed, too musky, too lush and exotic, to be taken seriously. Well, don't take it seriously then. Just have fun with it. I agree the perfume is pretty exotic, but when you can find a wine that fills the room with the scent of tea-rose in bloom, and has a waxy, broad texture that coats your mouth but brings a smile creeping to your face for the sheer joy of it all, well, I think that is a rare talent and I am unashamedly a Gewürztraminer fan. The wines are most famous from France's Alsace region on the border with Germany. Germany and Austria also grow Gewürz (as it is known), as do northern Italy and Hungary. In fact, most of Eastern Europe grows it. It's widely spread around the New World, but rarely shines. Perhaps it's not serious enough for them.

Viognier If you're in the mood for fruity wine – and I mean really fruity – Viognier is a shoo-in for you. The wine is golden, the perfume is like a late summer orchard full of apricots and peaches and the flavour is uncompromising. It's like a marvellous juicy fruit salad of peach and apricot, drizzled with honey, if you're lucky. It's not the wine to slurp back if you're thirsty (Sauvignon Blanc or Riesling would be better for that), it's not the wine to serve with your best slab of turbot (leave that to Chardonnay), but for an indulgent golden mouthful of fruit, Viognier is hard to beat. It used to be one of the world's rarest grapes, clinging on in a couple of vineyards in France's northern Rhône. Now it's found all over southern France, and Italy and Spain give it a go, along with Australia, South Africa, California – and Virginia, whose Viogniers can be world-beaters.

Fiano and its friends Fiano gives a marvellous, full-bodied, dry white wine in southern Italy, from Naples to Sicily. But it's just one of a host of old Italian white varieties that are now proving that Italian whites can be at least as exciting – and maybe more so – as Italian reds. Falanghina is another wonderful grape from near Naples – more scented, but equally good. Greco is another Neapolitan variety full of flavour. And the whole of Italy is waking up to the exciting potential of the native white grapes, from Carricante on the slopes of Sicily's Mount Etna, to the Garganega of Lake Garda in the north. So, though I chose Fiano to head this list, what it really stands for is the inspiring resurgence of whites the whole length of Italy.

Some tasty also-rans

Aligoté White Burgundy's forgotten grape, the embarrassing relation, the one they don't talk about. Well, even the most embarrassing dotty aunt can have redeeming features and Aligoté provides sharp, lemon and apple peel flavours in Burgundy's less good vineyards, and Eastern Europe and Russia make good use of it.

Colombard Colombard makes wines with tremendous, sharp, lime zest and green plum flavours in south-west France's Gascony. It's a sort of local Sauvignon Blanc. Since it wilfully hangs on to its fresh acidity in hot climates, Colombard is quite popular in parts of California, South Africa and Australia.

Malvasia The wine can be white, pink or red, sweet or dry, still or sparkling or fortified – what's going on? Well, the name is applied to loads of different grape varieties around the Mediterranean and out on the island of Madeira way out in the Atlantic Ocean (where it's called Malmsey). Since they're mostly not related, I can't generalize much, but there are some smashing sweet versions, mostly in Italy and Greece, some dull dry white ones and a delicious scented dry white from Croatia called Malvasija.

Marsanne You are most likely to see this variety's name on wines from Australia, or sometimes, California. But this honeysuckle and golden plum-scented variety is most important in France's Rhône Valley and Languedoc-Roussillon, either on its own or blended.

Muscadet As a pale, fairly neutral white wine from the mouth of France's Loire River near Nantes, this was an unlikely favourite in Britain for a generation or two. The grape is actually called Melon de Bourgogne, but no one cares that much.

Pinot Blanc A sort of milder version of Chardonnay; indeed, its wines were often called Chardonnay. It comes from Burgundy (as does Chardonnay) but most French examples are now from Alsace, where it makes creamy, appley, light whites and good fizz. Many parts of Europe – especially Germany and Italy – grow it, and the best New World producer is Oregon, USA.

Roussanne Bright, blossom-scented and most famous in France's northern Rhône Valley, but you rarely see the name on a wine label. They say it's not easy to grow, but there is quite a bit, almost always as part of a blend, in the Rhône and southern France, and occasional producers in Switzerland, California, Australia and elsewhere.

Sémillon From Bordeaux in south-west France, where it makes excellent, dry whites and the great sweet Sauternes, usually blended with Sauvignon Blanc. By itself it is usually waxy and broad, though when it's underripe, it's tangy and green like Sauvignon Blanc. Australia makes the most famous 100% Semillon wines – from the Hunter Valley where the wine somehow manages to transform itself from thin, pale lemon juice to toasted butter, nuts and lime zest over a decade or so. You can find it behaving in a fairly mild-mannered way in South Africa, South America and the USA.

Torrontés When I first came across this, I described it as 'celestial toilet freshener'. Wonderful, lime zesty, floral, heady, it could have deodourized most bathrooms. In fact, from the Argentine Andes it can be a delicious, refreshing wine. Uruguay also has a bit.

Verdejo Famous for producing one of Spain's fresh, sharp, leafy, grapefruity, dry whites at Rueda in northern Spain. Almost like Sauvignon Blanc – which is why it became a success. But that's about it for Verdejo, though a guy in Virginia is having a go.

Verdelho Most famous for making a fairly dry fortified wine in Madeira. Mainland Portugal makes nice dry white from it, but Australia (mostly in New South Wales and Western Australia) makes a more mouthfilling, oily, citrous, zesty, dry white version.

Verdicchio This is turning out to be one of Italy's best grape varieties for dry white wine, able to make powerful, savoury, satisfying dry whites under the names of Verdicchio dei Castelli di Jesi and Verdicchio di Matelica (both in the Marche). It appears as Trebbiano di Soave – in Soave – and as Trebbiano di Lugana, in Lugana.

Vermentino This is found in Italy around the Mediterranean coast and on Sardinia, though it is called Pigato in Liguria and Favorita in Piedmont. It generally makes fresh, citrous, apple flesh-flavoured dry whites, with a hint of wild herbs. It's popular in southern France, where it is often called Rolle, and on Corsica. The USA has a bit, as does Australia.

Vernaccia On Sardinia one variant of Vernaccia makes both pale dry whites and full-bodied dry or sweet sherry styles. At San Gimignano in Tuscany another variant makes lean, lemony whites, mostly popular because they're about the only local white on offer.

Viura Also known as Macabeo, this was thought to produce pretty neutral stuff in northern Spain and southern France. But it's the main grape in white Rioja, which can be very tasty; it's important in Spanish Cava fizz; and Roussillon in southern France makes some tremendous, dense, chewy examples, often blended with white Grenache and Carignan.

A QUESTION OF STYLE

Wine comes in dozens of different styles if we want to endlessly subdivide and subdivide. But I'll leave that to the geeks. I've outlined a dozen fairly broad categories to cover red, white and rosé wines so that you can have a better chance of choosing a style you're going to like. And don't forget all those wonderful fortified wines, and last but not least, there is sparkling wine, never last, never least.

MAIN RED WINE STYLES

Light and juicy Most wine areas produce something light and juicy for drinking young and lively without any thought of aging or classifying – without any thought of anything, really, except providing pleasure during the daily rituals of eating. Beaujolais in France is possibly the most famous. Loire Valley reds can do the same job. *Joven* or 'young' styles in Spain do a good job in areas like Rioja and Valdepeñas, and simple Garnacha is lovely in Aragon. Italy's Valpolicella and Teroldego do the trick. Young Chilean Merlot and Argentinian Bonarda can be delightful.

Silky, strawberryish This is the domain of the Pinot Noir grape. French Burgundy is the most famous example. Chile, New Zealand, Oregon, California and South Africa can also do it as can Romania. Some Spanish Riojas are oaky and silky, and some Bordeaux from St-Émilion and Pomerol are lush and, well, velvety rather than silky. A bit fuller, a bit thicker but still lush.

Chewy and blackcurranty This is the redoubt of the Cabernet Sauvignon. Some of these wines may be quite chewy as well as full of black fruit. Top Bordeaux Cabernet blends will get more of this flavour with age, though cheap ones probably won't. California, Australia, Chile, New Zealand and South Africa can do this, often blending the Cabernet with Merlot. Portugal's Douro is all kinds of dark fruits, often with scent. Italy's Tuscany – more dark fruits, often with added chew.

Warm and spicy Australia's Shiraz leads the way here, and Shiraz also delivers in varying degrees from Chile, South Africa and Argentina, though lush damsony Malbec is Argentina's main calling card. California's Zinfandel can be super-spicy. Southern Portugal, central and southern Spain, southern France and southern Italy all have loads of examples, and don't forget places like Lebanon – Lebanon almost invented the kasbah style of red wine – and Turkey.

MAIN WHITE WINE STYLES

Bone dry/neutral It doesn't sound all that attractive, but the majority of the world's whites are certainly neutral and in Europe most of them will be bone dry too. That's because so many basic whites are simply made to accompany snacks and tapas, hors d'oeuvres, nibbles

– call them what you will – and then to wash down the seafood and fish. Bone dry, neutral does quite a good job at that. French Muscadet used to be the most famous but nowadays Italian Pinot Grigio is better known, and most whites using local varieties from Portugal to the Eastern Mediterranean hit the spot. In the New World, unoaked Chardonnay or Chenin may fit the bill.

Green, tangy Sauvignon Blanc is the supreme grape variety here. Snappy, crunchy, zesty, zinging with acidity and green fruit flavours. New Zealand leads the way, but France's Loire Valley, Bordeaux and coastal Chile and South Africa can do cracking Sauvignon too. Otherwise Spain's Albariño and Rueda wines, Austria's Grüner Veltliner, Western Australia's Semillon/Sauvignon, and dry Rieslings in Australia, New Zealand, New York State, Germany and France's Alsace have a fair bit of zip.

Ripe, fruity With most Australian Chardonnays now being made much leaner and drier, it's more difficult to track down rich, ripe, fruity, dry whites. Chardonnay can still do it. California often sticks to this style, and cheaper examples from Chile, Argentina, New Zealand, South Africa and the Mediterranean countries will probably deliver. It's worth trying oak-aged South African Chenin and South Australian Semillon.

Aromatic There are a fair number of dry whites with rather alluring scents, as modern winemaking and earlier picking of the harvest points up perfume. The most famous and exotic will be from the Muscat and Gewürztraminer grapes (France's Alsace is particularly good at this), and southern Germany and Austria produce scented wines from grapes like Scheurebe, Grauburgunder (that's Pinot Gris/Grigio), and even Riesling. Other notable pot-pourris include Falanghina in Italy, Malagousia in Greece, Malvasia in Croatia, Torrontés in Argentina and Irsai Olivér in Hungary. North-west Spain's Godello is scented, Viognier should be lush and scented in southern Europe and the New World. England's Bacchus wine is redolent of spring hedgerows.

Nutty, intense Dry but succulent, subtle but intense, oatmealy, toasty, sometimes with a whiff of struck match sulphur (surprisingly delicious!). White Burgundy dominates this style, but it is increasingly being produced in Australia and New Zealand. South Africa can do it, as can California, Washington State and Oregon, and Canada. Parts of Italy do it well.

Golden, sweet Luscious mouthfuls, rich with honey, peach, pineapple and sometimes sweet citrus syrup. France's Sauternes is famous. Hungary's Tokaji is renowned. Excellent wines from Austria and Germany. Chile, Australia, California, New Zealand and South Africa all produce a few. Canadian Icewine is seriously rich.

MAIN ROSÉ WINE STYLES

How pink is pink?

Well, one thing needs saying right away – real men do drink rosé. It's become so popular with the brotherhood in some places, that people are talking of a 'Brosé' revolution. And another thing. Size does matter. I bet you have seen those gorgeous, inviting, lush-looking, big bottles of pink. Rosé magnums leap off the shelves, and at some parties you can hardly move for the piles of these elegant empties.

Rosé de Provence began it all. It doesn't do any harm that Brad Pitt and Angelina Jolie's Château Miraval makes the stuff. It doesn't taste of much, but it feels kinda nice and mellow going down, and its incredibly pale colour is decidedly alluring and sophisticated. Nowadays loads of people try to make this ultra-pale style but few can manage to make it with quite so little flavour. The rest of southern France and the Rhône Valley do pale, but with much more wallop. Every country makes some rosé and in cool northern Europe it is often more attractive than the same areas' attempts at red wine.

Mateus and Lancers from Portugal were the original pink fizzes. Pink sparkling wine is usually more expensive than the equivalent white fizz – especially in Champagne. Now that *has* to be because of how it looks in the glass.

Most New World rosé is a bit clunky. In places like South Africa and Australia that might have been because big macho wine beasts thought pink wine was beneath them. But maybe it's because most New World countries make red wines bursting with flavour and however hard you try to tame it down, there's just a bit too much fruit flavour for a successful, thirst-quenching pink.

Delicate Good rosé should be fragrant and refreshing, and deliciously dry – not sickly and sweet. France is good for this style. Bordeaux Rosé is attractive, slightly leafy tasting, while Bordeaux Clairet is a lightish red, virtually rosé but with more substance. Cabernet d'Anjou from the Loire Valley is a bit sweeter but tasty. Better still is Rosé de Loire, a lovely dry wine. Elegant Pinot Noir rosés come from Sancerre in the upper Loire and Marsannay in northern Burgundy. In the south of France Coteaux d'Aix-en-Provence, Lubéron and Ventoux produce plenty of dry but fruity rosés. Costières de Nîmes produces light, slightly scented styles. Côtes de Provence is dry, beguilingly smooth but often expensive. Bandol and Bellet on the coast of Provence are pricier still. Northern Italy produces light, fresh, pale rosé called *chiaretto*, from Bardolino and Riviera del Garda Bresciano on the shores of Lake Garda. Garnacha *rosado* from Navarra and Rioja in northern Spain is tasty, while English pinks are coming on nicely.

Gutsy Dry, fruity rosé can be wonderful, with flavours of strawberries and maybe raspberries and rosehips, cherries, apples and herbs, too. Most countries make a dry rosé, and any red grape will do. Look for wines made from sturdy grapes like Cabernet, Syrah or Merlot, or go for Grenache/Garnacha or Tempranillo from Spain's La Mancha, Campo de Borja and Jumilla. Puglia and Sicily in southern Italy make mouthfilling rosés, too. In the southern Rhône Valley, big, strong, dry rosés from Tavel and Lirac go well with food but drink them young at only a year or so old if you want a refreshing wine. South America is a good bet for flavoursome, fruit-forward pink wine – try robust Shiraz and Cabernet from Chile or Malbec from Argentina. Other wines include dry, fairly full rosé from California, often from Syrah, fruity Australian Grenache from the Barossa Valley or New Zealand pinks.

Sweet The original examples are Rosé d'Anjou (from the Loire Valley) and Mateus and Lancers rosé (from Portugal). Zinfandel from California, which is white with just a hint of pink and often described as 'blush' or White Zinfandel, is fairly sweet, but can be OK when chilled down to its toenails.

QUICK GUIDE TO FORTIFIED WINES

Necessity is the mother of invention. Fortified wines are wines that have had their alcohol levels considerably increased by the addition of high strength alcoholic spirit, either during the fermentation or soon after it. This has a massive effect on the flavour of the wine, but that wasn't the reason fortification was invented. It was simply a way to stop wine rapidly turning to vinegar, normally while being exported to markets in northern Europe – and, later, to America – by sea.

The two greatest fortified wine producers are Spain – for sherry – and Portugal – for port and Madeira. The basic table wine of Andalucía in south-west Spain, where sherry comes from, is white, feeble and pretty tasteless. The basic wine from the Douro Valley in northern Portugal, where port comes from, is dark red, rough, bitter and prone to sourness. Neither of these wines were attractive and centuries ago nor would they usually last the journey in barrel to northern European ports without turning to vinegar. But for various reasons, usually involving wars with the French, these wines were sent to northern Europe in vast quantities. And it was only when high strength brandy was added to them that they had the guts to survive the voyage.

MAIN FORTIFIED WINES

These can be startlingly dry or unctuously sweet.

Sherry The genuine article from Jerez in south-west Spain is the jewel for bone dry, sour yet creamy, nutty flavours in both pale and amber styles. These are some of the greatest bargains in the wine world.

Port The leading sweet red style, from the Douro in northern Portugal.

Madeira A fascinating, smoky, sweet-sour oddball from a magical island way out in the Atlantic Ocean.

Muscat wines The Mediterranean makes excellent Muscats in France, Spain, Portugal, Italy and Greece. Australia's Rutherglen Muscats are world-class and quite ridiculously sweet.

SHERRY

Sherry really is one of the great wines of the world. Nothing else tastes like sherry. Perhaps that's the problem: it's such a shockingly original flavour that most of us can't get to grips with it. This means that good sherry is remarkably cheap, and the small band of dedicated sherry enthusiasts get some of the best bargains in the wine world. Hopefully, the remarkable spread of tapas bars and Spanish restaurants outside Spain will give sherry's popularity a boost, but I wouldn't bank on it.

Sherry only comes from south-west Spain, and Jerez is the major producing town (the word 'sherry' is an Anglicization of Jerez). You used to be able to get Cyprus Sherry, South African Sherry, British Sherry (for goodness' sake!), but Jerez/sherry is a protected name now and only applies to the real stuff, from Spain.

The white Palomino grape provides the base for almost all sherry. Almost every great sherry is dry, starting with pale, tangy, fino and manzanilla. Proper amontillado is dry and nut brown. Proper oloroso is dry but deeper, intense in flavour and usually a blend of wines that can be 20, 40, 60 years old or even more. This blend is made by the 'solera' system, whereby banks of barrels are piled on top of each other. The bottom barrels hold the oldest wine, the top barrels the youngest. You draw wine off the bottom barrel and replace it with wine from the next barrel. You refill that one from the barrel above, the blends getting younger all the time, until you reach the youngest wine in the top barrel, and you top that one up with new wine. So the longer a 'solera' has been going on, the older the blend becomes. Finos and manzanillas are usually pale and quite young (just a few years old) but great olorosos might have a hundred different vintages represented in the blend.

There is a small amount of fine sweet sherry (*dulce* in Spanish) made using the Pedro Ximénez grape. This is dark and treacly and some of the richest wine on the planet. A lot of widely available sherry brands are vaguely sweet and inoffensive, to be kind to them. A modern invention, 'Pale Cream' is a sort of sweetened-up fino. A marketing man's delight.

Main sherry styles

Fino Fino sherries derive their extraordinary, tangy, pungent flavours from *flor*. Young, newly fermented wines destined for these styles of sherry are deliberately fortified very sparingly to just 15–15.5% alcohol before being put in barrels for their minimum of three years' maturation. The thin, soft, oatmeal-coloured mush of *flor (yeast)* grows on the surface of the wines, protecting them from the air (and thereby keeping them pale) and giving them a characteristic tang. The addition of younger wine each year feeds the *flor*, maintaining an even layer. Manzanillas are fino-style wines that have matured in the cooler seaside conditions of Sanlúcar de Barrameda, where the *flor* grows thickest and the fine, salty tang is most accentuated. True amontillados are fino sherries that have continued to age after the *flor* has died (after about five years) and so finish their aging period in contact with air. These should be bone dry and taste of raisins and buttered brazils. Medium-sweet amontillados are concoctions in which the dry sherry is sweetened with *mistela*, a blend of grape juice and alcohol.

Oloroso Sherry strongly fortified after fermentation to deter the growth of *flor*. Olorosos, therefore, mature in barrel in contact with the air, which gradually darkens them while they remain dry, but develop rich, intense, nutty and raisiny flavours.

Other styles Manzanilla pasada is aged manzanilla, with greater depth and nuttiness. Palo cortado is an unusual, deliciously nutty, dry style somewhere in between amontillado and oloroso. Sweet oloroso creams and pale creams are almost without exception enriched solely for the export market. Sweet, syrupy but frequently delicious varietal wines are made from sun-dried Pedro Ximénez or Moscatel grapes. A well-matured Pedro Ximénez sweet sherry is about as glutinously thick and mouth-coating as it is possible for a wine to get.

Other countries Although they can no longer call their wine 'Sherry', both Australia and South Africa make small amounts of outstanding sherry-style wines, usually in an amontillado or oloroso dry, intense style. Cyprus 'sherry' was never very good and has largely disappeared. British 'sherry' was a good deal worse and certainly should have disappeared by now.

PORT

For a long time the fortified port which was sent to Britain was strong and coarse – and dry. It was only due to a mistake by a producer up the Douro Valley who fortified his wine before the fermentation was finished, killing off the yeasts and leaving a lot of sugar in the wine, that sweet port became the norm.

Most port is based on a variety of red grapes, though there is some white port made – sometimes quite dry, and definitely a lot better now than it used to be. Some ports are drunk young (ruby), but most are aged either in bottle or in barrel.

Main port styles

Vintage This is the finest of the ports matured in bottle and comes from a single, outstanding harvest and from grapes from the best vineyards. Vintage port is not 'declared' every year (usually there are three or four declarations per decade), and only during the second calendar year in cask if the shipper thinks the standard is high enough. It is bottled after two years, and may be consumed soon afterwards, as is not uncommon in the USA; at this stage it packs quite a punch. The British custom of aging for 20 years or more for all its flavours and perfumes to develop can yield exceptional mellowness. Vintage port throws a thick sediment, so benefits from decanting.

Single quinta (Vintage) A single-quinta port comes from an individual estate (called *quinta*); many shippers sell a vintage port under a quinta name in years that are not declared as a vintage. It is quite possible for these 'off vintage' ports to equal or even surpass the vintage wines from the same house.

Late Bottled (Vintage) (LBV) Port matured for four to six years in cask and vat, then usually filtered to avoid sediment forming in the bottle. It is lighter than vintage port. It doesn't usually need extra aging after bottling but is still a dark red wine. Traditional unfiltered LBV has much more flavour and requires decanting; it can generally be aged for another five years or more.

Crusted This is a blend of good ports from two or three vintages, bottled without filtration after three to four years in cask. A deposit (crust) forms in the bottle and the wine should be decanted. A gentler, junior type of 'vintage' flavour.

Reserve Most can be categorized as Premium Ruby. They have an average of three to five years' age. A handful represent good value.

Ruby The youngest red port, with only one to three years' age. Ruby port should be bursting with young, almost peppery, fruit. There has been an improvement in quality of late, except at the cheapest level.

Tawny Ports aged in barrel are usually called tawny and are blends of many harvests. You don't have to mix it with lemonade any more to make it bearable. (The drink used to be called 'port and lemon'.)

Basic tawny is either an emaciated ruby, or a blend of ruby and white port, and is usually best avoided. Good ones are sold with an age designation on the bottle and are called aged tawnies. The wines are blends with a minimum average age, starting at 10 year old, where the wine may still have some red colour left and be a bit fiery. 20 year old tawnies are nutty, smooth and delicious, 30 year olds and the very rare 40 year olds even more so. Tawnies are the style most drunk by the Portuguese, and they don't feel shy about chilling them down for an hour or two in the fridge.

Colheita Tawny from a single vintage, matured in barrel for at least seven years – potentially the finest of the aged tawnies.

Rosé Usually very sweet and best served over ice or used in cocktails.
White Only the best ones taste dry and nutty from wood-aging; many
are coarse and alcoholic, and best served ice cold with tonic water
and a slice of lemon as an apéritif.

MADEIRA

Madeira is a Portuguese island way out in the Atlantic, which
produces a fortified wine that became famous because it was the last
port of call for ships leaving Europe and heading either to America,
southern Africa or the Indies. The flavour didn't matter; for the crew
this was the last chance for some grog before months at sea.

There are four main types: Sercial, which is very dry and fairly
acid; Verdelho – fairly dry but fuller and rounder; Bual – quite sweet
and brown; and Malmsey, the darkest brown and the sweetest. All
Madeira has an acid tang, however sweet, and usually also a very
individual smokiness which is deliberately produced in the wine to
mimic the effects of the long sea voyages which seemed to positively
improve Madeira during the age of sail. Though Madeira was popular
in northern Europe, the USA, in particular the southern States, has
always been regarded as the greatest Madeira connoisseur.

FORTIFIED MUSCAT WINES

Fortified Muscats are by far the most important of the other
fortified wines. They are made all round the Mediterranean basin,
with excellent ones in Greece (e.g. Samos and Santorini), Italy
(e.g. Moscato Passito di Pantelleria) and France (e.g. Muscat de
Frontignan and Muscat de Rivesaltes). Spain and Portugal make
good ones too (as Moscatel). South Africa has Vin de Constance and
Victoria in Australia makes the world-class Rutherglen Muscats.

QUICK GUIDE TO SPARKLING WINES

Sparkling wine exists to lift our spirits, to help us celebrate, to push
us all towards laughter and flirtation and fun. And it's the bubbles in
the wine which manage to do this, rather than the flavour. So how to
create the best bubbles really does matter.

CHAMPAGNE METHOD

Almost all the best bubbles are created by the 'Champagne' method
(it's usually called something like 'traditional' or 'classic' method
outside the Champagne region of northern France). This entails

filling a bottle with still wine, adding a mixture of yeast and sugar and banging on a crown cap. The sugar and yeast start a second fermentation, which creates a bit more alcohol, but a vast amount of carbon dioxide. Since the bottle is firmly sealed with a crown cap (that's the kind of cap you see on beer bottles), the gas can't escape. Luckily carbon dioxide is a very soluble gas and it all dissolves in the wine, waiting patiently for the moment you or I pour out this riot of foam and fun to get the party going.

Smaller bubbles This 'Champagne' method of creating a second fermentation in the bottle creates much smaller bubbles, in much greater numbers, than any other system, and in well-made Champagne-style wines, those bubbles can last up to 20 years.

Clearing the wine This second fermentation causes some yeast deposits in the bottle. These are removed by trapping them in the neck of the bottle, freezing this yeasty sludge, whipping off the cap and popping out the plug of sludge, then shoving a proper strong cork back in – and the wine will be clear and bubbly.

TANK METHOD

The next important method for creating fizz is called the 'tank' method. Here you put still wine into a large sealed tank and add yeast and sugar. A second fermentation erupts. The carbon dioxide is dissolved in the wine because the tank is sealed. Then the wine is drawn off and bottled with the bubbles still in it. But the bubbles are bigger, and there are fewer of them. A lot of cheap, dull fizz is made like this – it can be an OK drink if it's served virtually at 0°C/32°F. There are some good 'tank'-method bubblies, especially in Italy. Asti and Prosecco are both made like this.

BICYCLE PUMP METHOD

The worst – and I mean worst – way to make a wine sparkle – fitfully and briefly – is the 'bicycle pump' method, called *vino pompo* around the Mediterranean. Here, pretty filthy wine is literally pumped full of gas, which splutters momentarily in the glass, then leaves you with an unappetizing, fizz-free liquid you really don't want to drink. The only decent fizz made like this is some sparkling Sauvignon Blanc.

MAIN SPARKLING WINES

Good bubbles lift your spirits just by gazing at them in the glass. The world's most famous bubbly is Champagne from north-east France, but France's Crémant wines, Spain's Cava, Italy's Franciacorta, England, Australia's Tasmania, Brazil and northern California also produce lovely stuff, but can't use the name Champagne. Italian Prosecco is more party pop, as is German Sekt. Asti is a fruity Italian Moscato fizz from Piedmont, and Brazil does this style exuberantly.

IS CHAMPAGNE STILL THE BEST?

The first question is what is Champagne? All Champagne is sparkling wine, but most sparkling wine is not Champagne. Champagne is a region, based on the cities of Reims and Epernay north-east of Paris and the wine we call Champagne is the sparkling wine, made from three grape varieties (Chardonnay, Pinot Noir and Pinot Meunier), grown within this area. And the wine must be made to sparkle by inducing a second fermentation inside the bottle (see page 44).

A marketing success Champagne has been such a marketing success over the last couple of centuries that the word has almost become a generic term for fizz. Indeed, numerous countries called their sparklers Champagne without a second thought. But expensive lawyers working for the Champagne producers have tracked down just about everyone using the name and 'persuaded' them to desist. Nowadays, Champagne means sparkling wine from the Champagne region of France (although, surprisingly, some cheap bubbly in the USA is still called Champagne, but the expensive American stuff, including that from US outposts of big Champagne houses, isn't).

Until recently, most Champagne came from big companies (with big advertising budgets), big co-operatives or supermarket own labels. But global warming has affected Champagne and has meant that the grapes are now picked far riper than of old, and some of the most interesting wines now come from the grape-growers themselves, often in less well-known villages whose grapes had struggled to ripen before the climate began to warm up around the millennium.

The Champagne region There are three main areas: the Montagne de Reims, the Côte des Blancs ('The White Slope') and the Marne Valley, but there are also important vineyards further south, particularly in the Aube. Some of the vineyards are classified as Grand Cru (the best) or Premier Cru (the second best).

The Champagne grapes Champagne is made from white Chardonnay and black Pinot Noir and Pinot Meunier. You can make white wine from black grapes because the juice of black grapes like Pinot Noir is colourless (the colour in a pink or red wine comes from the grape skins, not the juice). Press the grapes gently and you get colourless juice. Most Champagne is a blend of black and white grapes. Blanc de Blancs ('white from whites') uses only Chardonnay. Blanc de Noirs ('white from blacks') is a white wine from the black grapes. The rosé usually comes from black grapes, but can use Chardonnay as well.

Vintage or not? Most Champagne is non-vintage – a wine based on one year's crop, but with older wines mixed in to soften and improve the flavours. A vintage wine has the year on the label and the wine comes only from that year.

De luxe cuvées These are expensive bottles, often of a fanciful shape, with fanciful names. Sometimes they're pricey but excellent – like Dom Pérignon or Taittinger Comtes de Champagne. Sometimes they're 'all sizzle and no steak' and for those with more money than sense.

Dry or sweet? Although Champagne is generally thought of as a dry wine, it does have a slightly complicated labelling code. 'Brut' is the typically dry wine we usually drink, but there are even drier wines, with titles like 'extra brut', 'brut nature', 'dosage zero' and so on. These are quite trendy and are usually pretty austere to drink. 'Extra dry' is, bizarrely, a bit sweeter than 'brut'. 'Sec' means off-dry, 'demi-sec' is slightly sweet and 'doux' is reasonably sweet.

OTHER CHAMPAGNE-METHOD WINES

But is Champagne still the best? It has come under increasing threat from sparkling wines from all round the world using the same classic 'Champagne' method and often from the same grape varieties.
England England is now producing significant amounts of highly individual fizz that can match Champagne in quality.

Crémant wines In France, Alsace, Burgundy, the Loire, Jura and a few other regions produce 'Crémant' wines (the word non-Champagne French producers have to use for 'Champagne'-method fizz), and it's often pretty good.

Cava Spain's Cava is quite different to Champagne, but good. Made throughout Spain but most comes from Catalonia.

Italy's sparklers Franciacorta from Lombardy near Milan is excellent and Trentino further north is very good.

Rest of Europe All the other wine countries produce bubbly, often using the 'Champagne' method. Much of it is good (especially in Austria and Portugal), but little of it is special.

Rest of the World The bigger quality threats to Champagne (apart from England) come from the New World. Canada makes small amounts of very good bubbly – some of it in chilly Nova Scotia. In the USA, Virginia and Michigan can make good fizz, as can mountainous New Mexico, and California, despite being a relatively warm climate region, does have some cool spots like the northerly Anderson Valley where excellent sparklers get made, often by offshoots of famous Champagne houses. South America has some good examples, though few excellent ones. Brazil is probably the best performer. South Africa has suddenly leapt forward and is making substantial amounts of really good sparklers. Australia takes fizz very seriously and now that much of the base wine comes from Tasmania, has some very fine examples. New Zealand has one or two stars (such as Cloudy Bay's Pelorus) but given its cool conditions it should really be offering us more.

OTHER SPARKLING WINES

There are some lovely bright sparklers that are made using the cheaper 'tank' method to create the bubbles.

Italy's Prosecco and others Italy, in particular, does this simpler, fresher style of sparkling wine very well. The most famous example is Prosecco from the north-east, a fruity, easy-going bubbly which has taken the wine world by storm – simply because it is such a delightful party pop. A wine that used to be thought of as Italy's party pop is Asti from the north-west. This is sweeter and fruitier than Prosecco (it's made from the very aromatic Moscato grape), and it's lower in alcohol. Chill it right down and it's a delight. And a third delightful fizz is Lambrusco – real Lambrusco with a cork in the bottle, purple-red, slightly sour and chewy, foaming and not quite dry. Try *that* with a spaghetti ragù.

Sekt and other wines Germany makes a lot of Sekt (usually by the 'tank' method) and if it's fresh and zippy it can be good, but too much of it is off-dry, earthy and acidic. Southern Russia makes some pretty decent stuff too (by both 'tank' and 'Champagne' methods). The Russians invented a 'double-quick' method of making wine sparkle called the 'continuous' method. Portugal also makes some use of this.

There is a large amount of cheap fizz in the USA, most of it not very good (oh, all right, pretty terrible). Without doubt, the American country that does party pop best is – Brazil. Of course! There are some excellent 'Champagne'-method wines, but the carnival spirit is fed by oceans of delightful, Asti-style fizzy Moscato.

WHAT IS A CLASSIC WINE?

'Classics' usually refers to something pretty old, something that has proven itself over time, maybe over hundreds of years or more. Something given respect for the unique position it holds. And something that people are likely to use as their template, their example when they need something to copy.

So, to be a classic it's pretty important that people have heard about you. In the world of wine that means that you haven't just spent centuries making the locals blissfully happy, yet you're completely unknown any further away than the next town. You need to have had an influence through trade, through politics, through art and religion on the cultures you come into contact with. And you need to be still around. The classic wines of Ancient Greece and Rome got lost in the Dark Ages. No one really has much idea what they were like. Only one or two of the modern wines of Greece and Italy have had any influence outside their own countries.

The main areas for classic wines that have influenced the rest of the world are Germany, Portugal, Spain and, above all, France. France is brilliantly situated at the crossroads between southern and northern Europe. She has always traded with her neighbours and back in the Middle Ages was exporting her best wines from Bordeaux to the English and Dutch. Also, France is perfectly placed by latitude – between about the 50th and the 43rd parallel north – to be an ideal spot to allow numerous grape varieties to achieve perfect ripeness – not overripe, not underripe, just... ripe.

We often think of the best wines as being primarily made from just a single grape variety. In Burgundy this is true – Pinot Noir for red, Chardonnay for white. But there are many examples of when it is the blended wine that gives the best results. So here are a few of the 'classic' wines that have had the biggest effect on the entire world of wine on every continent where the wine grape will grow.

CLASSIC WINES

France/Bordeaux Surrounding the Gironde estuary and the city of Bordeaux, this large region produces the most classic red wine style of all, based on the Cabernet Sauvignon and Merlot grapes. These wines have been traded around the world for a thousand years. Whenever new producers in new regions wish to emulate a wine style, red Bordeaux is their most frequent choice. Bordeaux red wines almost always use two and can use five or six grape varieties – Cabernet Sauvignon and Merlot are the main ones, often blended with Cabernet Franc, Petit Verdot, Malbec or Carmenère. Dry white Bordeaux is usually Semillon blended with Sauvignon, while Sauternes, the most famous sweet white style in the world, also comes from here.

France/Burgundy Made in small quantities, but with huge renown, these wines come from the east side of France, south of Dijon. Burgundy is famous for the world's greatest dry whites using the Chardonnay grape. The style is copied worldwide. Burgundy also produces the world's most tantalizing, silky reds from Pinot Noir, and red Burgundy styles using Pinot Noir grapes are possibly the biggest challenge for any winemaker. They all want to make great Burgundy. Few succeed.

France/Champagne The entire culture of sparkling wine comes from this chilly French region to the north-east of Paris. Some Champagnes are from a single variety – Blanc de Blancs is from Chardonnay – but most fizz also includes the black Pinot Noir and Pinot Meunier grapes to make a black grape/white grape mix, even though the wine is usually white. Using a method of making wine sparkle which entails setting off a second fermentation inside the bottle (a risky business in the old days), Champagne has been copied everywhere anyone makes fizz, from California to Tasmania.

France/Northern Rhône The areas of Côte-Rôtie and Hermitage make memorable red wines from Syrah. They've been doing so since Roman times but because the amounts were tiny, hardly anyone knew about these wines. Now they do and ambitious winemakers worldwide use the Syrah grape. Australia makes an especially rich type of Syrah which they call Shiraz. Many people copy them too, so that's a sort of 'New Classic'. The northern Rhône uses only Syrah for its red wines, but the southern Rhône Valley, stretching down to the Mediterranean, has a number of varieties that do well – Grenache is the most important, along with Syrah, Cinsaut and Mourvèdre. The famous Châteauneuf-du-Pape wine is allowed to use 13 varieties – and one property, Beaucastel, actually does. White Rhône wines can be a blend of several varieties including Roussanne, Marsanne and Viognier.

France/Sancerre Frankly, this isn't really a classic wine because, although they've been making wine here forever, Sancerre only became famous about 60 years ago as a wine to sell to thirsty Parisians. Sancerre is a little town in France's eastern Loire Valley and at a time when nearly all the world's everyday white was thick and dull, Sancerre made bright, light, fresh, fruity dry white. The secret? The Sauvignon Blanc grape. New Zealand nicked the idea of Sauvignon in the 1980s and now everyone wants to copy New Zealand. But the mouth-watering Sauvignon wine we so enjoy today all started here in Sancerre.

Italy Most of Italy's 'classic' wines have hardly been copied elsewhere. Barolo from the Nebbiolo grape and Brunello and Chianti from the Sangiovese grape are natural classics with few imitators. Valpolicella's dense, dark 'Amarone' is beginning to be copied. Fizzy Asti has spawned excellent sweet Brazilian fizz, and the Prosecco style is spreading.

Spain/Sherry Sherry is a dry fortified wine from Spain. This has sadly rather gone out of fashion, but there have been periods between the 16th and 20th centuries when sherry was the world's most popular wine. Sherry is a dry, nutty wine fortified with brandy, initially to make it strong enough to survive a sea voyage, but mostly because it allowed a light, neutral white wine to undergo an astonishing transformation in barrel and become one of the world's most original experiences. If you haven't tried dry sherry – pale or amber – you really should: there's nothing like it. All around the world winemakers have tried to copy the style. Only the Australians and South Africans have had much luck.

Spain/Rioja Rioja is actually an imitation of Bordeaux wine but is a big success in its own right. Made largely from Tempranillo grapes, but many of the best ones also include Garnacha, Graciano and Mazuelo.

Portugal/Port If sherry is the great dry fortified wine, port is the great sweet one. Port is made in the Douro Valley – a bewitchingly beautiful World Heritage site. Dozens of different grape varieties grow there, and port is virtually always a blend. The most important varieties are Touriga Nacional, Touriga Franca, Tinta Roriz and Tinta Cão. Usually made from black grapes, large amounts of high strength alcohol spirit are added to stop the fermentation, which leaves about half of the intensely sweet grape juice unfermented. And that's the sweetness in the wine. Port can be purple, red or palest amber in colour (and, occasionally, white) and is generally strong and swooningly sweet. It has been copied worldwide. The South Africans and Australians have had most success.

German Riesling Riesling grapes are native to Germany, and when grown on the banks of the Rhine or Mosel rivers they can produce wines of unparalleled delicacy, often dry, sometimes slightly sweet, occasionally very sweet. Because of the cool growing conditions, and the long sunny autumns, German Riesling can be ripe at very low alcohol levels, especially in the Mosel Valley, and its side valleys, the Saar and Ruwer. Such wines have a high, mouthwatering acidity and piercing citrus fruit. Those from the Rhine Valley (the Rheingau, Nahe, Rheinhessen and Pfalz regions) will be fatter and more peachy in flavour.

German wines fell from favour towards the end of the 20th century, but their Riesling is still regarded as the leader, and worldwide copycats include France (in Alsace), Australia, New Zealand, South Africa, New York State and the West Coast of the USA.

Hungary Tokaji is remarkable Hungarian sweet wine, which no one has yet managed to copy, and I'm not holding my breath.

New World The red Bordeaux blend of two to six grapes is widely copied, but Cabernet Sauvignon-Merlot is the most generally employed. Americans have the title 'Meritage' for these Bordeaux blends. The white Bordeaux blend of Semillon-Sauvignon is pretty popular. You may see SGM on a label – that stands for Syrah, Grenache, Mourvèdre, the southern Rhône blend and the basis for Châteauneuf-du-Pape red wines.

WHAT IS NEW WORLD WINE?

What *is* the New World? Basically it covers the leading non-European producers – the USA, Australia, New Zealand, South Africa, Chile and Argentina. New World also suggests an attitude in winemaking that maximizes the use of modern technology and science and which puts the customers' preferences before any commitment to a traditional style of wine production and wine personality.

Why do New World wines taste like they do? Where did they get their ideas from? The most fundamental difference between Old, i.e. Europe, and New World wines has always been that the New World wines are riper, have more fruit and are often a better drink by themselves, whereas with Old World wines you often seem to need a bite to eat for them to show off their charms.

Most New World countries didn't really have a wine tradition and those that did, like South Africa, weren't making much that was drinkable. They didn't have decent grape varieties, and didn't know much about what vineyard conditions would produce the best quality. For that matter, what *was* the best quality?

Exactly. That's where the Old World was so important. And nowhere more so than the Bordeaux and Burgundy regions of France. For centuries these two areas had been thought of as producing the finest reds and whites in the world. Powerful red Bordeaux, more delicate red Burgundy and supremely full-flavoured but savoury, nutty, white Burgundy. These were the ruling champions of world wine, with perhaps a nod to the dry whites of Bordeaux and the Loire Valley.

So when the New Worlders, above all the Californians, then the Australians, wanted to create their own high-quality wine cultures, these top French wines were what they looked to. They didn't have the same growing conditions in the Americas or Australasia, but they could import the same grape varieties and they could ape the winemaking practices of the Old World. The Californians led the way and copied the very best methods of Bordeaux and Burgundy, planting the same grapes and employing such methods as aging wine in new oak barrels, which give rich vanilla and spice flavours to the wine.

That's why the New World was dominated by Cabernet Sauvignon and Merlot reds (from Bordeaux) and Chardonnay whites (from Burgundy). The next wave was white Sauvignon Blanc (from Bordeaux and the Loire Valley) and red Pinot Noir (from Burgundy) and, because of its juicy, jammy richness, Shiraz (the Syrah from France's Rhône Valley). One non-French exception is Germany's

Riesling. This was taken to Australia by German settlers in the 1840s and, in very different conditions, managed to become Australia's leading quality white wine over the next century. Winemakers are always trying to get Riesling going in the coolest areas. New York State and Canada, not surprisingly, are successful, as are, sporadically, New Zealand, South Africa and Chile.

Why weren't the New World wines made from Italian grapes like Nebbiolo (Barolo) and Sangiovese (Chianti), or Spain's Tempranillo (Rioja)? They weren't famous enough. Chianti and Rioja were well enough known, but not as world-beaters. The French won that battle hands down.

ONE GRAPE OR TWO OR EVEN 12?

If you ask a wine drinker, which is better? A wine from a single grape variety, or a blend? They'll usually answer that the single variety wine is best. Yet if you ask a winemaker, the majority will say that a blend is superior to a single variety wine. There are some varieties like Riesling and Pinot Noir where varietal purity is virtually a religion and blending is rare – and even more rarely confessed to. But most grape varieties make a more interesting, rounded, attractive wine by having a bit of this and that blended in.

Bordeaux is the greatest example of this. The New World has adopted Cabernet Sauvignon as its red grape of choice. Yet none of the great red Bordeaux wines are made from unblended Cabernet Sauvignon – there's always some Merlot added, and usually several other grape varieties as well. Merlot, too, is wildly popular around the world, yet in its homeland of Bordeaux is virtually always blended in to provide more interesting wine. And nowadays, throughout the New World, you'll find wines labelled 'Cabernet Sauvignon' or 'Merlot' because that's what the wine drinkers want. But the tastiest examples will usually be blended with something else. It's easier to understand a wine labelled simply by its grape variety, it's the easiest way to predict what flavours you will probably get. But maybe it's time to move out of your comfort zone and start drinking blended wines – the Mediterranean lands are full of them, and the wines' flavours may be less precise, but they might be more challenging and satisfying.

LOW-ALCOHOL WINES

Wine by definition is an alcoholic drink. There are various scientific ways to reduce the alcohol to less than 0.5%, but I've never had an example that tasted remotely like real wine, and would probably prefer to drink mineral water. Partial alcohol reduction is more successful, and more natural since some wine styles have always been created by stopping the fermentation before it is finished, leaving sweetness and, often, bubbles in the wine. Italy's Moscato d'Asti and genuine Lambrusco are two delicious examples.

QUICK GUIDE TO 'GREEN'

The first thing to remember about the following styles of wine (organic, biodynamic, natural and orange) is that the wines won't necessarily taste better than more traditional wines, indeed, they may taste worse. So the real reason for drinking, say, organic is partly to do with your own health, since there is likely to be less use of additives – even generally beneficial ones like sulphur – and partly to do with the health of our planet, because the fewer artificial and chemical substances we add to our vineyards the better. That's not really in doubt.

ORGANIC WINES

We're all now familiar with the concept of organic because all the major food retailers have been offering organic vegetables, organic fruits and, more recently, organic meats, cheeses, pastas and goodness knows what. The message of organic is simple. Organic culture is better for the soils of our planet, and creation of foods from organic ingredients is better for us. To be honest, no one is quite sure about the second assertion – there are many modern, positively industrial methods that do no harm to us and there are numerous chemical and scientific additives which do us no harm either.

But the tide is flowing in favour of organic, especially in a world swirling with the effects of global warming and pollution. So, even though wine drinkers traditionally have been strangely unconcerned about organic practice (quite possibly because so many of the wines were more expensive and less enjoyable than conventional offerings), people are finally beginning to demand organic wine. And the realm of organic wines now spreads across the world and encompasses very big companies, not just hipster smallholders.

In simple terms, organic vineyards are ones that don't use any manmade fertilizers, fungicides, pesticides or herbicides, and ones that definitely don't contain anything that has been genetically modified. In warm, dry areas, it's not that difficult to grow grapes organically, but in cooler, wetter areas, where vine diseases like mildew and rot are threats, it's much more difficult. For this reason, both sulphur and copper sulphate are allowed to combat vine disease, though there are now many naturally derived oils and teas that are used. Changing the way you prune and shape your leaf canopies can help, and some growers are developing friendly fungi and bacteria to attack the diseases that threaten their crop.

Organic wine is basically wine from organic grapes, and sulphur is allowed to be added in the winemaking process, albeit at relatively low levels (sulphur is the most efficient antioxidant known to man, and has been for 2000 years). In the USA and Canada, 'organic wine' means no sulphur has been added, 'wine made with organic grapes' means some sulphur additions in the winery are allowed. And by the way, organic doesn't guarantee that a wine is vegan, because some animal and fish derivatives are allowed to help settle the wine's sediment in the vat or barrel.

BIODYNAMIC WINES

Biodynamic vineyards use all the concepts of organic, but take things further. Indeed, many critics of biodynamism call it a 'cult' or a 'hoax'. Yet many of the best producers in such French classic areas as Burgundy, Alsace and the Loire are devotees and make superb wine. So what *is* biodynamics?

Well, all synthetic additives in the vineyard are banned (except, once again, sulphur and copper sulphate, though growers may decline to use these). The health of the vineyard is looked after by the application of various plant and mineral teas and preparations, as well as the use of natural composts in the place of fertilizers. The preparation of teas involves numerous dilutions, and stirring in one direction then the other, so that you've got a kind of homeopathic solution which is then sprayed on the vines in pretty small amounts. All vineyard work must be done according to a lunar calendar based on the signs of the zodiac, whose four main divisions for vineyards are described as root, leaf, flower and fruit days. Different sorts of work needs to be done on different sorts of days. You can see why the sceptics scoff.

And they scoff further when followers of biodynamism seem to suggest that the rural dimension of their beliefs is more important than the flavour in the bottle. One leading exponent has as his motto 'Before being good, a wine should be true'. So making the best-tasting wine is not the main point. To be honest, if it weren't for the fact that many highly intelligent winemakers make fantastic wine by biodynamic methods, you'd be right to scoff. And many less talented winemakers may have ethically pristine vineyards and wineries, but their wines taste of the mud and winery floor rather than the moral high ground that they expound.

NATURAL WINES

This is a relatively recent phenomenon. If biodynamic means organic+, 'natural' means organic on steroids. Which is an unfortunate analogy since these guys really don't like any chemical additions at all (including sulphur if possible). The purpose is to authentically and utterly express the 'sense of place' of each particular wine, using grapes grown at very least organically, fermenting the juice without any help from commercial cultured yeasts (vineyards are full of wild yeasts and they argue that these give a purer flavour. Well, sometimes…), and processing – ooh, that's rather an industrial term – without chemical, and frequently mechanical, help of any sort.

This movement started in France's Beaujolais as a reaction to that wine's over-commercialization and, more recently, has found fertile ground in the Loire Valley and the Jura wine regions, where 'natural' wines have helped to give an identity to the wines of many small growers who were virtually operating under the radar, and probably finding it pretty difficult to make a living. Various other parts of Europe, notably the non-classic areas of Spain and some of northern Italy, and some New World areas, like bits of South Australia and the Maule region of Chile, have fostered 'natural' wine movements, with varying levels of success.

And here's the thing. In a few cases these noble aims seem to produce limpid, piercing, thrilling wines of unexpected flavour and tremendous energy, often at low alcohol levels. Which is truly exciting. Far more often the wines are unfocused and surprisingly flat, and fairly frequently they verge on the cloudy and the sour. All in the name of 'natural'.

Now, if 'natural' wine is a movement, I'm all for it. If 'natural' wine adds another dimension, another nuance, another dynamic to our wide and exciting world of wine, I'm all for it. But the danger is that 'natural' wine producers and devotees are increasingly likely to discuss any wines that are not 'natural' as toxic, an affront to nature, an abomination to the moral order – all that guff. They should wise up. 'Natural' wine is a welcome extra strand of experience to make the enjoyment of wine ever more fascinating. But an ideology that says 'we are natural' and you by implication are unnatural is an unwelcome and untruthful nonsense.

ORANGE WINES

'Orange' wine is an interesting but challenging oddity. These are wines made from white grapes, but, instead of the juice being quickly pressed off the skins and then fermented separately, with 'orange' wines the juice is fermented on the grape skins, along with the pips, and sometimes the stalks too. The wines have an unusual personality, chewy and bitter from the tannin in the pips, skins and stems, and with flavours more to do with sap and earth and dried-out fruits and herbs than the typical fresh modern whites. The colour can be orange, but doesn't have to be.

This is the style of wine that has been made in Georgia (in the Caucasus) for 8000 years. And it's an acquired taste, being bitter and savage, not at all fruity and likely to have a strong taste of the chewy grape skins and either the earth of the vineyards or the clay of the clay pots traditionally used for the fermentation and aging. Georgia prefers to call these wines 'amber', not 'orange', and they're also often described as 'Qvevri' wines after the local name for the clay fermenting jars.

'Orange' wines can be rather wonderful, though you'll need to be sitting down when you first try them, and I don't blame you for being upset if you get served an 'orange' version of, let's say, a Sauvignon Blanc or Pinot Grigio in a bar without being warned about what you're buying. A surprising number of wineries round the world are now making examples – often just flirting with the idea, not including the stems, just leaving the skins and juice together for a few weeks – but, so long as you know what you're ordering, the 'orange' wine movement is at very least interesting.

Wines from Georgia produced like this have made such wines fashionable, and 'orange' wines have been made in Friuli in northeast Italy since 1998. Slovenia and Croatia have been making versions for almost as long. Many countries are now having a go, often with excellent results. But they're not like your average House White.

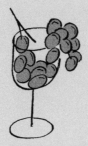

FROM GRAPE TO GLASS

Work in the vineyard follows a basic pattern the world over, but the timing of each stage is dependent on both the local climate and the weather conditions of the year. Even though the style and quality of the wine is inherent in the grape, the winemaker can do plenty to improve upon the raw material and the huge amount of money being invested in new wineries all over the world suggests that key choices are being made at the winemaking stage.

Although winemakers love to say that the wine is made in the vineyard, it is a bit more complex than just finding a nice piece of land, planting some grapes, waiting around blithely while they ripen – then you just pick 'em, crush 'em, ferment 'em and bottle 'em. A few 'back to the future' primitivists do pretty much just that. But there are really quite a lot of activities, from winter pruning right through to bottling, that make a big difference to how your wine will taste, So here are some key points in the vineyard and in the winery if you are making a red, pink or white wine. And I discuss one or two interesting topics like climate change as well.

A YEAR IN THE VINEYARD

Winter The leaves fall, the sap descends and the vine becomes dormant. Pruning can be done at any time during the winter.

Spring The sap starts to rise, and the first signs of growth appear: the young vine must be protected against frost from now until early summer. Sprays may be necessary to protect the buds against pest and disease, though organic and biodynamic growers use other methods. Ploughing and hoeing aerates the soil and clears weeds; fertilizer may be applied. As the ground warms up, new vines can be planted. Once the vines begin to shoot, the new growth needs to be tied to the wires, otherwise the foliage would shade the fruit and prevent it from ripening; the final trellising takes shape.

Summer Eight weeks after budbreak, the vine flowers for about 10 days and then the fruit sets; cold or wet weather at this time can cause poor fruit set and thus reduce the quantity of the harvest. Summer pruning, or leaf plucking, may be necessary to allow more sunlight to reach the fruit. At *veraison* (the point at which the fruit changes colour) a green harvest may be done to reduce the size of the crop, and superfluous clusters removed. Netting or bird scarers may be used to protect against bird damage.

Autumn Picking usually begins in September/October in the northern hemisphere, and February/March in the southern, but climate change is bringing these dates forward.

CLIMATE CHANGE

Climate change means the world is warming up. So what will that mean for wine? It is going to make life hardest for wine regions that already have pretty hot climates. For instance, inland Australia. Climate change means temperatures have been rising there every year, and annual rainfall is lowering. This is making life increasingly tough for producers and if the trend continues could radically affect Australia's ability to produce most of the wine it churns out today – and certainly the styles will change beyond recognition. Equally though, other areas will open up.

Take England. It's never had enough reliable sunshine to ripen grapes properly, but change is in the air and the wine industry, especially for sparkling, is growing, even blossoming, and stunning the wider wine world with its quality every year. Scandinavia next.

TERROIR

This is a word you might hear cropping up when the wine chat gets going. What does it mean? It's a French word. 'Terre' is the French for earth. So, basically terroir is the earth the wine comes from, the vineyard that the wines grew in. But that's only part of the story. There are loads of types of soil, and loads of types of subsoil, and different grape varieties prefer different soils – some like clay, some gravel, some like limestone and so on.

The scientists say the minerals can't affect the flavour of the wine because a) they have no flavour and b) there is no way mineral molecules could transfer a flavour into the juice of the grape in any case. Fair enough. But wines do taste of what I *think* are minerals or soil – slate maybe, or gravel washed by rain, or fresh midsummer earth dampened by morning dew, or chalk, or granite – yes, I know, there's no scientific support, but the flavour in wine is all about suggestion, association, ephemeral fleeting memories of emotion or place, of sound and colour and touch, and these do have a smell. And I know that this Chardonnay can't really taste of baked bread because there's no bread in it, and this German Riesling can't really taste of slate, because slate hasn't got a taste. Yes. Indeed. But that Chardonnay stirred a memory in my mind of a particular loaf of bread at a particular time. That Riesling had a mineral austerity that made me think – if slate had a taste, it *would* taste like this.

Wine is about borrowed flavours. It has no taste language of its own. But the indefinable sensations you can only half describe can often be most easily dealt with by putting them down to the influence of terroir. Does that make any sense? If a wine has a muddy taste and we say, oh, it's the terroir – I doubt it. It's probably just a rubbish wine. But if we say: the composition of the soil, the height of the vineyard, the angle to the sun, the effect of every drop of rain, or ray of sunshine or puff of breeze during a vineyard's year – could *that* put a unique thumbprint on a wine? I'd say yes. And the passion, the commitment, the vision of flavour of the people who cultivate those – is that also terroir? Absolutely. Without them, terroir is just the potential of a particular piece of land. With them, that potential is triumphantly realized. Indeed, if you have an identical piece of land but six different winegrowers, you'll get six different wines.

MAKING WINE: RED, WHITE OR ROSÉ?

Red wine Red grapes are usually crushed and may be wholly or partly destemmed. (Grapes which are not destemmed undergo what is called whole bunch or whole berry fermentation.) The juice is fermented with the skins and (if wanted) the stems in vats of wood, cement, fibreglass or stainless steel, sometimes in small barrels, sometimes in cement 'eggs' or amphorae. Chaptalization – that's adding sugar to boost the sweetness which the yeasts can work on, and so boost final alcohol levels – or acidification – if the juice is too flabby or soft – may be done at this stage.

During fermentation the skins and stems rise to form a layer, or cap, on top of the fermenting must or juice. This layer must be kept broken up and in contact with the must if colour and tannin are to be extracted. The usual method is to pump juice over the cap (*remontage*). Alternatively, the cap may be punched down (*pigeage*) either manually or mechanically. In some cases it is trodden, by human foot or mechanical foot. The skins and juice, and the stems if present, are left to macerate after the end of fermentation, to extract more colour and tannin. The wine is run off the skins into wooden barrels or into vats made of stainless steel, cement or fibreglass. The skins are pressed to extract all the liquid; this is called press wine. It will be matured separately and blended in later, if required.

Rosé wine Made either by fermenting the juice of red grapes with the skins for a brief period, until the desired degree of colour is obtained, or by blending red and white wine (with the major exception of Champagne, this method is illegal in most of the EU, but with the advent of pink Pinot Grigio, pink Prosecco, and the libertarianism of Vin de France, I suspect that from now on, anything goes).

White wine White grapes are destemmed and crushed. Occasionally skins and juice are left in contact for a short period to extract flavour from the skins, but overdoing this can release harshness. So usually the destemmed grapes go straight to the press, which separates juice and skins. The juice is fermented in wood, stainless steel, cement or fibreglass. Chaptalization or acidification may be done at this stage.

The new wine is run off into wooden barrels or into vats made of stainless steel, cement or fibreglass.

Final stages of winemaking The wine may undergo malolactic fermentation. This changes the sharp-tasting, malic 'green apple' acid that all wines have to the rounder-tasting, sometimes creamy lactic acid, but if you want to keep the zing in a wine, you stop the 'malolactic' from happening.

While the wine is maturing in vat or barrel, the fine lees (the dead yeasts left from fermentation) may be stirred periodically (*bâtonnage*), because they have a creamy, nutty flavour which dissolves in the wine. Lees add texture and taste. If you want the wine simple and fresh, don't leave it on the lees. You may see the term 'sur lie' on France's Muscadet wine labels – this will signify a gently dry, soft white. Some New World white producers also mention it on the label, or back label.

Alternatively, the wine may be racked off its lees by being run from one barrel or vat to another. All the vats or barrels are tasted, and the final blend put together. The wine may be fined and/or filtered and/or cold stabilized to remove impurities. It is then bottled.

Sweet wine Good sweet wine may be made by stopping fermentation at the desired balance of alcohol and residual sugar, either by adding sulphur to kill the yeasts, or by centrifuging the wine to remove the yeasts. But the best sweet wine comes from grapes that are naturally high in sugar. Here, the fermentation may stop by itself before all the sugar has been turned into alcohol because the yeasts can't work at high alcohol levels, usually around 15% alcohol. All the remaining grape sugar is left in the wine as natural sweetness. This is what happens with wines like Sauternes or Tokaji.

OAK

Just about every wine drinker in the land has an opinion about oak. And that opinion used to be – yum, I just love that spicy, creamy oak richness. But now it's more likely to be – yuck, I can't stand that spicy, creamy oak richness. What's going on? Don't worry, it's just the pendulum of fashion swinging. Wooden barrels and vats were, until relatively recently, the usual receptacles used for fermenting and aging wine. Oak was the wood normally used, though some countries have traditions of using other woods like acacia or chestnut.

To make a barrel, you chop down a mature oak tree – it could be one or two hundred years old – and cut the wood into straight staves which you then have to bend into a barrel shape. You do this by placing the staves round a hot fire and using the heat to bend the wood into the barrel shape. The heat will also draw out all the oils and essences in the wood, and they'll caramelize in the flames.

So the inside of your barrel will have a nutty, toasty-tasting coat of things like vanillin drawn out of the wood. If you then fill the barrel, either with grape juice which will then ferment, or with wine which sits there for months on end, these spicy, nutty, vanilla-like flavours will dissolve in the wine. And that's what gives the oaky taste.

Most of the top red and white wines in the world either ferment or age – or both – in barrels. And the oak adds lots of extra flavours. Interestingly, as the wine world moves away from intensely oaky flavours, big barrels are being favoured because they add less taste to the wine. The traditional barrel is 225 litres (often called the Bordeaux barrel or *barrique*). We are now seeing many more larger barrels of 300 and 500 litres.

Oak aging doesn't work very well on cheap wines, because the wine is often too neutral and all you taste is oak. New World Chardonnays can be the worst offenders, but you'll also find many red Merlots, Cabernets, Shirazes and Spanish Tempranillos that overdo the oak. And with cheap wines the oakiness may not come from a barrel at all. A winemaker can buy oak essence, oak grains or chips, and oak staves – all of which add oaky flavours to a wine while it sits in a stainless steel vat. It doesn't taste as good as oakiness from a barrel, but it saves a lot of money. On the other hand, white Rieslings never taste of oak, Sauvignon Blancs rarely do, and there is now a whole raft of wines from such countries as Italy, Slovenia, Croatia and Greece that use their own native grape varieties, and don't employ oak barrels.

Elsewhere, there is a move towards using old oak barrels. These are barrels whose flavours have already been dissolved by the wine, so they're pretty neutral. But because wood provides a gentler environment than stainless steel for producing wine, many winemakers think they create their purest, most expressive (i.e. tasty) wines using old wooden barrels.

QUICK GUIDE TO COUNTRIES

By quick, I do mean 'quick'. I'm just going to flash through the main countries, giving you a fleeting look at the kind of wines they make. It won't be comprehensive; it's just so that if you're sat in a bar or stood facing a wall of wines in a supermarket, this is vaguely what you might find.

THE EVER WIDENING WORLD OF WINE

When you think that wine can just about be made in both Finland and Norway, that vineyards are now flourishing in England, Denmark, Holland and Russia, that every country south of there until well into the Tropics is making wine, and that the same pattern is occurring in the southern hemisphere – well, you'll see why we need a country guide. Climates and soils are different and the grape varieties that will ripen successfully are different. And all these factors make for completely different flavours in the wine. But this is a 'quick' guide, so I will just focus on a few which I think are particularly important. Hmm. I don't know. I'm such a supporter of the underdog, I think I will sneak in as many as I can find space for. Just a few lines or two – for now. But a generation ago New Zealand and Argentina and England would only get a line or two. Where are the next star producers going to come from? Probably among these fringe producers of today.

FRANCE
The world's most famous winemaking country and still on top

France doesn't necessarily produce the most wine – that's normally Italy's job – and it seems to be going through a crisis of confidence at the moment as even the French are giving up wine-drinking in droves. But it is still – always has been – the most influential wine-producing country, and it does still – always has done – produce a larger amount of really tasty, distinctive, and frequently brilliant, wines than any other nation on earth. (Sorry, Italy.)

Quick guide Champagne for sparkling wine in the north. Bordeaux for red and white, pink and even sparkling, in the South-West. Bordeaux is probably the most famous wine region in the world because it produces more tiptop reds – based on the Cabernet Sauvignon and Merlot grapes – than anywhere in the world. It's also a producer of wonderful dry whites using Sauvignon and Sémillon grapes and, using the same grapes, superlative sweet Sauternes. The rest of the South-West has many pockets of good wine – Bergerac, Monbazillac, Cahors, Madiran and Jurançon lead the way. Burgundy in the east is famous for reds from the Pinot Noir grape and whites from Chardonnay. The Rhône Valley flows south from Lyons and is basically a superb red wine region with pockets of fabulous white.

But there are more excellent regions in France. Alsace, on the German border in the North-East, produces lush, scented, but dry whites (and a little red). The Loire Valley produces the whole gamut of red, pink and white, dry, medium and sweet, still and sparkling. Its most famous wines are Sancerre, Saumur, Vouvray and Muscadet. To the east, the Jura and Savoie are both high quality, low volume producers. The whole of the southern seaboard, from the Italian border to the Pyrenees, is a wine nirvana. Provence is most famous for rosé, but produces lots of other stuff, too – Bandol, on the coast, can produce some of France's most fascinating reds. If you're in the area, try the white wines of Cassis, a fishing port near Bandol, and a good match for the local seafood. The Midi or Languedoc-Roussillon, which starts west of Marseille and spreads right round to Perpignan and the Spanish border, is France's biggest wine producer. Much of the wine is pretty basic, but there are dozens of pockets of high quality. Here are a few: Pic St-Loup, Minervois, Faugères, Limoux, Corbières, Côtes du Roussillon-Villages, Collioures and Banyuls.

ITALY
Great quality at every price point, from world class classics to hidden gems

Italy has as many fascinating wine styles as France, but they are less well known, and have had little influence on winemakers in the rest of the world. Also the modernizing revolution, which can make lovely, refreshing drinkable wines out of almost any grape varieties, started much later in Italy than it did in France.

Quick guide The whole country grows grapes, right up to the Alpine passes of Aosta in the North-West. But the most famous wines of the North-West are the sturdy, challenging and occasionally brilliant red wines of Piedmont, south-east of Turin. Barolo and Barbaresco are the best-known reds; Nebbiolo, Barbera and Dolcetto the most important red grape varieties. Gavi is the best-known white; Arneis and Cortese are important varieties. Fruity Asti fizz using Moscato grapes also comes from Piedmont. The city of Milan is more a wine drinker than wine producer, but Italy's best dry sparklers come from nearby Franciacorta.

The North-East has a wide array of wine styles. North of Verona the Alto Adige and Trentino regions produce super fresh reds, whites and sparklers. Verona is home to Bardolino and Valpolicella reds (including the tremendous, mouthfilling Amarone) and dry white Soave. Over towards Venice and Trieste, there are vineyards on all sides, many producing Pinot Grigio and Prosecco, and Friuli, on the Slovenia border, makes some very serious wines (mostly white).

The centre of Italy is dominated by Tuscany and the cities of Florence and Siena. Tuscany is the redoubt of the Sangiovese red grape and its most famous wines are Chianti (especially Chianti Classico), Brunello di Montalcino and Vino Nobile di Montepulciano. The previously mosquitoey area of Bolgheri in western Tuscany is now a trendy red wine producer. The best whites come from Verdicchio on the east coast, and Orvieto down towards Rome. Vin Santo is a rare but ravishing sweet delight.

The south starts below Rome (whose local wine is the rarely inspiring white Frascati), but by the time you get to Naples, things get much more exciting. Campania is home to some of Italy's most fascinating new wave whites from very old grape varieties like Fiano, Falanghina and Greco, as well as the rip-roaring red Taurasi. Puglia, the heel of Italy, was seen as the place to plant vast vineyards of the 'international' varieties like Chardonnay and Merlot. But Puglia's glory is in its plantations of old varieties like Primitivo and Negroamaro.

Sicily was once thought of merely as a supplier of cheap bulk wine. It has now reinvented itself as the creator of some fascinating reds and whites based on old varieties, and the vineyards around Mount Etna are now almost too hipster for their own good, but pale reds from Nerello Mascalese and tingly whites from Carricante are genuinely individual. The Nero d'Avola black grape is also full of character elsewhere in the island. Marsala used to be a famous fortified wine produced in the west of Sicily. Sweet wines from the small islands of Lipari and Pantelleria are exciting and very individual.

Sardinia is an island with a lot of vines. Most of the best wines are rich, chunky reds from Cannonau (better known as Grenache or Garnacha) or Carignano. We hardly ever see these wines off the island.

SPAIN
With more land under vine than any other country, Spain produces traditional styles as well as exciting modern wines

It doesn't seem that long ago that when we thought of Spain we just thought of Rioja and Cava fizz, with a few of us also pitching in with sherry. How things have changed. Spain is now one of the most vibrant wine producers in Europe, with exciting stuff going on in every part of the country.

Quick guide The North-East is still dominated by Cava but also has world-famous Priorat just south-west of Barcelona. Catalonia has quite a few interesting reds, and further inland delicious old vine Garnacha reds pop up in Calatayud and Campo de Borja. Next to them, you've got Navarra and, just south of Bilbao, Rioja. Although Rioja is mostly known for oak-aged reds, there are some tasty, juicy young '*joven*' styles. Pinks and whites can also be really good.

North of Madrid, Ribera del Duero uses Tempranillo to make some of Spain's greatest reds, and Tempranillo also makes chunky reds in Toro near the Portuguese border. The Mencía grape is a rising red star in the North-West. Rueda is a dry white area, but the most exciting whites in Spain are coming from Galicia in the North-West where Albariño (in Rías Biaxas) and Godello (in Valdeorras) excel.

The bulk of Spain's wines come from the south – La Mancha is a vast region south of Madrid and vines spread right across to the east coast at Valencia and further south. Most of these are powerful reds. The south-west region of Andalucía is dominated by Jerez (sherry) north of Cadiz, with similar wines being made in Montilla-Moriles.

And don't forget the islands. The Balearics (particularly Mallorca) and the Canaries (particularly Tenerife) are starting to produce some fascinating reds from little-known grape varieties.

PORTUGAL
For such a small country, Portugal makes a diverse range of wines, from traditional port and Madeira to exciting original reds

Portugal is a very exciting wine country and one of the reasons is that she mostly uses her own indigenous grape varieties, rather than the international ones like Cabernet Sauvignon and Chardonnay (although there are good Portuguese examples of both). But this has hampered Portugal's exports since the grape varieties are unfamiliar to most of us. Never mind, Portugal is a country that will massively reward efforts to understand the wines.

Quick guide The far north has two diametrically opposed wine styles: light, tangy, snappy Vinho Verde and rich, sumptuous sweet port (see page 41). The Douro Valley, where port is made, is also a source of fantastic dry reds and good whites. South of the Douro, Dão and Bairrada do serious reds, and there are numerous wines, mostly to the north and east of Lisbon in Lisboa and Tejo, which are tasty and affordable – and usually red. Just south of Lisbon there's some delicious Moscatel at Setubal, and the hot parched inland region of Alentejo towards Spain is particularly good for reds. The Algarve in the south has lots of vineyards and should make pretty tasty stuff but rarely does. Madeira, an island way out in the Atlantic, makes small amounts of exceptional fortified wines.

GERMANY
Stunningly beautiful vineyards producing some of the world's greatest and most elegant whites

Germany has some of Europe's most hauntingly beautiful vineyards, and also some of Europe's most hauntingly beautiful wines. The Riesling grape is a German variety, famed for its ability to achieve a delectable ripeness at a low alcohol level, and a high acid level. Usually this is a recipe for tart thin wine, but not in Germany. Riesling wines are made in every style, from bone dry to some of the sweetest in the world, but many of the greatest wines leave some fruit sweetness in them, usually balanced by thrilling, mouthwatering acidity.

Quick guide The vineyards are mostly in the centre and south of the country, though there are a few vines in the former East Germany. And most of the vineyards are clustered along the banks of the river Rhine and its tributaries. The Ahr Valley is the northernmost of these, making tangy Riesling and surprisingly good pale red Pinot Noir. The Mosel is probably the greatest German exponent of the fruit/acid/perfume balance which Riesling elsewhere often promises but rarely achieves.

Along the Rhine, the Mittelrhein has some marvellous steep, stony vineyards which produce just about enough to slake the thirsts of tourists visiting the Lorelei Rocks. The Rheingau is serious Riesling country, making a wide selection of wines from dry to sweet, but usually marked by a mellow ripeness and subtle minerality. Just south of the Rheingau is the delightful Nahe, and east of the Rhine is the challenging but fascinating region of Franken where Silvaner challenges Riesling as best grape variety.

South of Frankfurt and Mainz, the style of whites becomes much broader, often earthier, less finely focused and in Rheinhessen, Pfalz and Baden, Riesling shares the vineyards with various other whites like Pinot Blanc (Weissburgunder) and Pinot Gris (Grauburgunder). But, more importantly, there has been an enormous increase in red wine plantings, led by Pinot Noir (Spätburgunder) but also including grapes like Dornfelder, and there are even patches of Cabernet Sauvignon and Merlot. Württemberg, near Stuttgart, specializes in pale red Trollinger, but can make good Pinot Noir.

AUSTRIA
Elegant wines, from minerally whites to luscious sweet styles

Austria's wine business was wrecked in 1986 by a scandal involving anti-freeze. But instead of rolling over and withering away, the scandal galvanized what had been a rather lazy, unambitious wine culture into becoming what is now one of Europe's most dynamic. Austria makes every type of wine from feather-light whites to succulent golden sweeties, and pale reds from ethereal to full-on powerhouses. But the best wines, red and white, are those that continue to reflect the temperate northern conditions that Austria possesses in abundance.

Quick guide The Riesling thrives along the Danube, particularly in the Wachau. The indigenous Grüner Veltliner flourishes all over the country but especially along the Danube and its tributaries. Excellent sweet whites are made along the muggy, humid banks of the Neusiedler See, Europe's shallowest lake. The best reds are made from the local Zweigelt, Blaufränkisch and Sankt Laurent grapes. Steiermark (Styria) in the south makes surprisingly lean whites.

SWITZERLAND
Plenty of impressive wines based, unsurprisingly, on French, German and Italian styles

It's easy to overlook Switzerland as a fantastic wine producer because so little of the wine ever gets exported. But there's a flourishing wine culture in this Alpine redoubt, with both reds and whites capable of great things. Chasselas is the most widely planted white grape. In France and Germany it is dismissed as a feeble grape, but the Swiss make wines of a duck down softness and mountain meadow freshness that are an absolute delight.

Quick guide The Vaud, near Lake Geneva, is the main region for Chasselas and also grows a lot of red Gamay and Pinot Noir. The Valais, just to the south-east of Lake Geneva, is Switzerland's most exciting region, and its vineyards, clinging to the mountainsides, are breathtaking. It's in a very dry rain shadow (with way less rain than Bordeaux, for instance). Crucially, most of Switzerland's really ancient grape varieties grow here, and there is a heart-warming determination not to let them die out. It's worth looking out for Petite Arvine, Humagne Blanc or Païen (whites), as well as Cornalin and Humagne Rouge. But the majority of the plantings are the French classics led by Pinot Noir, Gamay and Syrah (reds), with Chardonnay, Pinot Gris and Marsanne (whites).

There are also some pleasant light wines made in western Switzerland, near Lake Neuchatel, and in eastern Switzerland near the German and Austrian borders. In Ticino bordering Italy, Merlot is the dominant red.

NORTHERN EUROPE

The most important of the European countries north of the 50th parallel of latitude is England, because of its remarkable progress in making tiptop sparkling wines (as well as some good still whites). Belgium, Holland and Denmark all produce some nice light whites, and you can find wine as far north as Sweden (quite good), Norway (well, OK …) and even Finland (hmm …).

ENGLAND
The tiny wine industry has come of age and produces world class wines, especially fizz

It used to be the easiest way in the wine world to get a laugh – start extolling the virtues of English wine. Oh, how they would chortle! And they had a point. Until the 1990s hardly any English wine was more than a curiosity to be drunk if you had no other choice. But the 1990s brought several pioneering sparkling wine producers to the fore – led by Nyetimber, Breaky Bottom and Ridgeview – and from a tiny base English sparkling wine has become a real force in the world of quality. Investment by Champagne giants Taittinger and Pommery in English vineyards will surely be followed by others as Champagne inexorably warms up and their leading producers seek out cooler conditions. It helps that the soils of southern England are frequently the same as those of Champagne.

Quick guide Most of the important developments and higher quality wines have come from the counties south of London – Kent, Surrey, Sussex, Hampshire and Dorset. The North and South Downs provide two ridges of pale chalk soil – perfect for vines – but there are also ridges running between the Downs, usually on clay and greensand soils, which have produced some of England's best grapes. Essex is a dry county, and grows a lot of excellent Bacchus and Pinot Noir. Suffolk may soon follow suit. The most important Midlands vineyard is Three Choirs in Gloucestershire, but vines thrive as far north as Yorkshire, as well as in Wales, Devon and Cornwall to the west. Scotland has had a go and the whisper is that even Northern Ireland is pondering establishing a walled vineyard near Strangford Lough – one of the mellowest climates in the whole British Isles.

EASTERN EUROPE
A mixed bag but there are some decent wines

Some of these countries don't really like being called Eastern Europe any more because of the ex-Communist overtones, but that's where they are. Some countries have become – or returned to being – serious wine players. Some are still a bit peripheral.

The Czech Republic and *Slovakia* Both make some decent wine, but neither shine. The white is better than the red.

Hungary Hungary is famous for the great classic Tokaji sweet wine made from nobly rotted or botrytized grapes, but there are also good whites from wonderful grapes like Furmint, Hárslevelű and Szűrkebarát (oh, all right, that's actually Pinot Gris, but the Hungarians do it very well), as well as red Kadarka and Kékfrankos. You'll find some pretty good Cabernet Sauvignon, Chardonnay and Sauvignon Blanc too.

Romania The country's long wine tradition is slowly reviving, but at the moment Romania is the source of much of Europe's tastiest, low-priced Pinot Noir and Pinot Grigio.

Moldova Excellent vineyards that used to produce thrilling reds, and the winemaking industry is gradually getting back on track.

Ukraine Hit by the loss of Crimea, its most important wine region, to Russia in 2014, but makes good reds down on the Romanian border.

Bulgaria Used to be a very important supplier of bargain Cabernet and Merlot, but, with a few exceptions, is still struggling to carve a quality niche for itself.

Slovenia Adjoining Italy, Slovenia makes considerable amounts of very tasty whites and some good crisp reds.

Croatia Makes wonderful white Malvasija and fresh bright reds in Istria, on the Adriatic Coast, as well as beefy reds from the breathtakingly beautiful vineyards of the Dalmatian Coast, and succulent whites from the Danube basin.

Serbia, Macedonia and **Montenegro** There are signs of good wines.

THE EASTERN MEDITERRANEAN
From ancient Greek wine styles to modern world class reds

Greece For so long thought of as merely the provider of holiday plonk and that acquired taste – Retsina. There's a revolution going on as the Greeks rediscover their own old grape varieties, red and white. Look out for white varieties like Assyrtiko, Moschofilero and Malagousia, and Xynomavro and Agiorgitiko reds. Sweet Muscats are often superb.

Cyprus In the far eastern Mediterranean this island is also attempting a wine revolution, though her native grapes are less exciting than those of Greece.

Syria Not surprisingly, the country's wine industry is tiny.

Lebanon A thriving wine culture mainly in the Bekaa Valley; the best wines are spicy, chocolaty reds and are often world class.

Israel Fine wine is being made in the cooler regions (Upper Galilee, Golan Heights and Judean Hills). There are good Bordeaux-style reds, Syrahs and dessert wines; many of these, but not all, are kosher wines.

THE MIDDLE EAST AND ASIA

From the Transcaucasus and the origins of wine to China, the modern super-hero showing the rest of the world what can be achieved in only a few years

We sometimes need to remind ourselves that most of the earlier evidence we have for the development of a wine culture is from the Middle East, and in particular the area from eastern Turkey across to Georgia and down to the Tigris and Euphrates Valleys.

Turkey A relatively thriving wine industry, based substantially in the western end of the country but with its most interesting vineyards in the east, where political disruption makes life difficult, to say the least. The Turkish government doesn't exactly encourage the wine industry either.

Around the Black Sea North and east of Turkey, both ***Armenia*** and ***Azerbaijan*** produce wine, but ***Georgia***'s wine culture is much more robust, not surprising since this is where the most ancient wine artefacts so far have been found. Some wines are still made in ancient clay jars called Qvevri, very much like they were made 8000 years ago. They're weird, earthy, bitter, but strangely exciting. Southern ***Russia***, along the Black Sea coast, also has a thriving wine culture, now augmented by that of the Crimea.

Asia There are wines of quite good quality being made in central republics like ***Kazakhstan*** and a certain amount of reasonable wine in places like ***Thailand*** and even ***Bali***. ***India*** is more important, with significant vineyards in Maharashtra inland from Mumbai and Karnataka north of Bangalore.

Japan A fair amount of wine is produced but its very humid climate makes ripening most varieties a problem. The prefectures of Yamanashi, Nagano and Yamagata on the island of Honshu are the main vineyard areas. Koshu is a Japanese variety that makes a popular, extremely mild and delicate wine style.

China A quick learner, China has shot to the fore as a grape grower and wine producer and now has the third biggest vineyard area in the world. Various ancient varieties are cultivated, but the growth is most marked in Cabernet Sauvignon and the other Bordeaux red varieties. Conditions are not generally easy. The main regions are Shandong, south-east of Beijing, Hebei and Shanxi, south-west of Beijing and Ningxia, in the centre of China, north-west of Xian. Xinjiang is an area of extremely cold winters and hot summers in the far north-west. Yunnan is a very promising region in the Himalayan foothills to the far south. Nearly all the best Chinese wines so far have been red (red is the colour of good luck in Chinese culture), and most of these are based on the Cabernet Sauvignon grape.

AFRICA
South Africa is carving out an exciting, innovative future in wine

All the countries of northern Africa bordering the Mediterranean, from Egypt to Morocco, have significant vineyard plantings, but currently produce little wine of any great excitement. There are vineyards in the most unlikely places elsewhere in Africa, such as Ethiopia, Tanzania and Namibia, but South Africa is the only world-class producer on the continent.

South Africa Wine has been made in the Cape since the 17th century and in Constantia (also called Vin de Constance), a sweet wine made on the slopes of Table Mountain near Cape Town, they had a world-beater as long ago as the 18th century. So you could say that South Africa has the oldest wine tradition in the New World. But actually the tradition that is now making real waves with wines of imagination, individuality and beauty didn't really get going until the end of apartheid in the 1990s.

Centred on Stellenbosch, which produces superb Cabernet Sauvignon, Chardonnay and Chenin, high-quality wine production has spread out, up the windy, chilly west coast, into the parched but high potential granite and shale soils of the Swartland and down to the far south, through the old apple county of Elgin on to Overberg, Walker Bay and Cape Agulhas at the very tip of Africa. There are numerous other vineyard plantings, some big, like Robertson, some small like Citrusdal Mountain and Cape Peninsula.

Whites and reds are of equal quality – Sauvignon Blanc and Chardonnay lead the whites and Cabernet and Shiraz the reds. Pinot Noir, Grenache and old bush vine Cinsaut are also doing well. There is some smashing fizz, as well as some serious fortifieds.

California dominates American wine production, but every state now has at least one winery making wine

Grapes are grown in varied conditions, from Washington State in the north-west to Texas in the south and Long Island on the Atlantic seaboard. Not every state grows grapes, even though they all have at least one winery – I'm not sure what Alaska's wineries use, but if it's locally grown, it sure isn't wine grapes.

California California dominates American wine production, so let's deal with that first. Napa Valley is the most famous area, just north of San Francisco, and Napa Cabernet Sauvignon is probably America's most famous wine. But there's a lot more to the United States – and to California – than Napa Valley Cab. Sonoma is between Napa and the Pacific Ocean and manages to make just about every style of wine, from rich Zinfandel to fragile Pinot Noir, and Anderson Valley, further north, foggier, cooler, more challenging, produces fabulous fizz and fine Chardonnay and Pinot Noir.

Inland from San Francisco, the San Joaquin Valley (also called the Central Valley) produces vast amounts of generally dull wine, but Lodi, at the northern end, grows some very nice stuff. Further east, the Sierra foothills are famous for very old, gnarly Zinfandel vines. South of San Francisco, grape growing is more fragmented, Santa Cruz and Livermore being the most exciting at the bottom of San Francisco Bay. Further south, the Salinas Valley is a bulk producer, but with excellent vineyards on the valley slopes, especially on the south side. Paso Robles is hot and wild and then we suddenly tumble into a bunch of cool-climate areas famous for Pinot Noir and Chardonnay based on San Luis Obispo, Santa Maria Valley and Santa Ynez Valley just north of Santa Barbara. There are a few vines in Malibu (yes, really!) and further south, but that's about it.

Oregon The exact opposite of California – a wet, windy, positively European climate. That's what attracted a bunch of radicals to try to make French-style Chardonnay and, particularly, Pinot Noir. Pinot Gris and Pinot Blanc have also made their mark. The major vineyards for these varieties are clustered in the Willamette Valley south of Portland, the capital. Further south, the Rogue and Umpqua Valleys are warmer and more likely to boast Cabernet Sauvignon.

Washington State Most of the vineyards here operate in virtual desert conditions to the east of the Cascade Mountains and are clustered along the banks of the mighty Columbia River – right down to the Columbia Gorge near Portland, Oregon. Yakima is also a very important wine area, as is Walla Walla even further east, some of whose best vines actually grow just over the border in Oregon. Dark, ripe reds from Merlot, Cabernet Sauvignon and Syrah are the speciality, but good Chardonnay, Viognier, Sémillon and even Riesling are quite common.

Idaho A slightly more extreme version of Washington State, but can produce good, snappy reds and whites and very good fizz.

South and Mid-West **Texas** makes a bit of wine and some of the stuff from the High Plains area is pretty good. **Arizona**, **New Mexico** and, especially, **Colorado** are surprising successes in the South-West.

North Central The most successful state, despite challenging growing conditions, is **Michigan** with some excellent fizz and Riesling.

New York State A well-established wine industry in the Finger Lakes region, up towards Lake Ontario, with exciting Rieslings the main item. Long Island is more recently established but produces high-quality Chardonnay, Merlot and Cabernet Sauvignon.

Virginia All the eastern states have some wineries, of wildly varying quality, but Virginia has a proper high-quality wine industry making waves with wines as diverse as excellent Viognier, Petit Manseng, Cabernet Franc, Petit Verdot and even Nebbiolo (usually only at home in Piedmont in north-west Italy).

Canada Sweet icewine is the wine that made Canada famous, but she now produces light, elegant, cool-climate reds from Pinot Noir and Merlot and savoury Chardonnay, spicy Pinot Gris and crisp Riesling. The two most important regions are the Okanagan Valley in British Columbia and the Niagara Peninsula in Ontario. The sparkling wine, especially from Ontario and Nova Scotia, is increasingly good.

Mexico Mexicans have never really taken to wine. The few quality vineyards are mostly in the Baja California peninsula.

SOUTH AMERICA
Fruit, flavour and value for money are the reasons behind the success of winemaking on this continent

South America's healthy, sun-soaked vineyards can produce large amounts of decent wine at a low price. But nowadays the leading countries are making superbly individual wines in national styles as different from each other as those made in European countries.

Chile South America's leading wine country, with vineyards as far north as the Atacama Desert, 1770km/1100 miles north of Santiago, way down to Patagonia over 640km/400 miles south of Santiago. Initially, the varieties planted were mostly red – Merlot, Cabernet Sauvignon and Carmenère – and the vineyards were in the Maipo and Colchagua Valleys in the Central Valley south of Santiago.

But Chile has a very long coastline fronting icy cold Pacific waters, and has managed to create numerous cool-climate regions like Limarí, Leyda and Aconcagua Costa, where a wide variety of white and red varieties ripen perfectly. Tremendous Chardonnays and Sauvignon Blancs share the honours with exciting Pinot Noirs and Syrahs. In the south, in Maule, Itata and Bío Bío, old bush vines are now being lovingly nurtured and are producing exciting reds and whites. And País, the variety originally planted by the missionaries in the 16th century, is at last being shown respect and making delicious, gentle, fruity reds.

Argentina The country took longer than Chile to modernize its wine world, but is now able to punch its weight with a wide variety of reds, led by Malbec and Cabernet Sauvignon, and fresh, exciting whites, primarily from Chardonnay and the florally scented Torrontés. Whereas Chile can create cool conditions by hugging the sea coast, Argentina has to climb up towards the Andes, and some of the world's highest vineyards (including for now the absolute highest, in Salta) are in Argentina. Mendoza is the main centre for wine, and look for the sub-regions of Uco Valley and especially Tupungato and Gualtallary. Patagonia also has some good vineyards.

Uruguay The best wines are red, often using the Tannat grape, and her most exciting vineyards are to the east, towards the Atlantic at Rocha and Maldonado.

Brazil Most of this vast country is unsuited to grape-growing. Exceptions are the tropical São Francisco Valley in the northeast where vines can give two crops a year, and the far south of the country around Serra Gaucha. Good red wines are possible, especially in the high Planalto Catarinense, and the Serra do Sudeste down near Uruguay. Brazil also produces excellent sparklers, in particular delightful frothy sweet Moscatos.

AUSTRALIA
A huge range of climates leads to wines of every style imaginable, now copied around the world

Australia has probably done more than any other country to fuel the New World wine revolution. They are the great democratizers of wine. And that reflects what life's like in Australia, too. It's the only country that I know where you can expect a knowledgeable discussion about serious wines with your taxi driver on the way in from the airport. South Australia is the country's wine powerhouse, but the states all have different strengths and styles.

Western Australia The Swan Valley, near the capital, Perth, was one of the first areas of Australia to begin winemaking in 1834. Vineyards were established there because they're close to a major city with its thirsty inhabitants, not because the conditions were ideal (as happened also in the Hunter Valley north of Sydney). It's pretty hot in the Swan Valley and high-quality winemaking has since moved further south.

Margaret River is now the most famous area, established primarily by a disparate bunch of doctors in the late 1960s and '70s. This narrow strip of land pushing out into the Indian Ocean is often described as being as close as Australia can get to the conditions in France's Bordeaux region. Certainly, Margaret River makes tremendous red Cabernet blends and white Semillon-Sauvignon Blanc blends but it also produces pretty exciting Chardonnay. Elsewhere in Western Australia, vineyards are scattered but excellent wines come from the cool Manjimup, Pemberton and Great Southern regions.

South Australia Home to many famous big wine brands, much of whose fruit is grown in the hot, dry, irrigated Riverland zone on the banks of the Murray River. But South Australia also has various, very different, high-quality areas for wine. Clare Valley, well north of Adelaide, is famous for Riesling, but also does good Shiraz and Cabernet Sauvignon. Barossa Valley, closer to Adelaide, is most famous for Shiraz from ancient vines, but also excels at Grenache and Cabernet. The Eden Valley in the hills above Barossa is a little cooler, and produces some of Australia's most fragrant Rieslings and Shiraz.

The Adelaide Hills hold what are probably the state's coolest vineyards and they make excellent Sauvignon Blanc, Chardonnay, Pinot Noir and Shiraz, while McLaren Vale, south of Adelaide, is warmer and best for richer reds. Langhorne Creek produces large amounts of soft red wines. The cool Limestone Coast at the southern tip of the state is producing really exciting wines, led by Coonawarra – famous for Cabernet Sauvignon – Padthaway and Wrattonbully.

Victoria Probably has more variety than any other state, but many of the growing areas are very small. The main areas are the two famous cool zones near Melbourne – Yarra Valley and Mornington Peninsula – and the warm fortified wine specialist Rutherglen in North-East Victoria. But there are numerous other small areas, usually on the cool side, producing fabulous, scented, cool-climate Shiraz and Pinot Noir, along with numerous whites, and some good fizz. Areas to look out for are Beechworth, King Valley, Geelong, Heathcote, Bendigo and Grampians. Victoria also produces large volume wines on the Murray River.

New South Wales The most famous area is the Hunter Valley, north of Sydney. Frankly, this subtropical mixture of sun and storm, downpour and drought, is a pretty tough place to grow anything, but with Sydney as the local market, some superb Shiraz and Semillon have been produced over the years. And this is where the Rosemount and Tyrrell's companies started the Australian Chardonnay Revolution. Of various other wine areas up in the Dividing Range Mountains, the best are Orange and Canberra District, around the capital city that produces some thrilling, cool-climate flavours, especially with Riesling and Shiraz. The volume-producing region is the Riverina, on the Lachlan and Murrumbidgee Rivers.

Queensland There is not an awful lot going on wine-wise, though the Granite Belt, right on the New South Wales border, can produce some sturdy red stuff and quite fresh whites. South Burnett, north of Brisbane, isn't bad either.

Tasmania This island is making the biggest waves from a pretty small crop of excellent grapes. Initially dismissed as too cold for anything but apples, then dismissed as just about OK to provide the acid base wine for fizz, Tasmania is now not only providing most of the best fizz in Australia, but also exceptional Chardonnay and Pinot Noir still wines, as well as some real surprises from Cabernet and Shiraz/Syrah. Global warming does have a few things to make us grateful for.

NEW ZEALAND
Classic whites and refined reds, all singing with vibrant flavours

For such a tiny country off by itself in the Southern Ocean, New Zealand has had a remarkable effect on our wine-drinking world. You can sum it up in two words: Sauvignon Blanc. Or maybe three words: Marlborough Sauvignon Blanc. The Marlborough region in New Zealand's South Island virtually invented the tangy, zesty, citrous and green apple flavour of modern white wine when it produced its first Sauvignon Blancs in the 1980s. The whole world has been copying New Zealand's white wine style ever since. The reason its white wines are so thrillingly thirst-quenching is because it's pretty cool down in New Zealand's south (the Antarctic isn't that far away). So wines retain their freshness. But New Zealand isn't just about Marlborough, or Sauvignon Blanc.

South Island Marlborough, at the northern tip, is New Zealand's biggest wine region by far, and by far its most famous. Renowned for Sauvignon Blanc, it does other whites very well and is increasingly good at fizz and Pinot Noir and it's just started dabbling with Syrah. Nelson and Waipara both make fine whites and some wonderfully individual Pinot Noir reds while Central Otago, way down in the snowfields of the far south, makes intense Pinot Noirs and good whites.

North Island A little warmer than the South. There are several excellent areas. Martinborough and Wairarapa inland from Wellington make very good Pinot Noir – the region is now called Wellington Wine Country. Hawkes Bay on the east coast grows excellent reds from Syrah and the Bordeaux varieties, particularly from the warm Gimblett Gravels zone. Gisborne, a little further north, is famous for very tasty Chardonnay. Waiheke Island out in the Gulf of Auckland makes superb reds and whites.

PRACTICAL STUFF

WHAT THE LABEL
TELLS YOU

What do you need to know about
a wine from the label? Where it's
from, what grape variety it's from,
who made it, how old it is. That's
just about it. New World wine labels
mostly try to make this pretty clear.

HOW TO DECIPHER WINE

When you come to choose a wine, the grape variety is almost always centre stage, because we buy most of our wine according to what grape variety the stuff comes from. In many European countries – particularly France, Italy and Spain – wines are labelled according to *where* they come from, though in most areas you are only allowed to use specified grape varieties, so once you learn what grows where, you'll know which variety goes into your wine. Red Bordeaux will be Cabernet Sauvignon and Merlot, Rioja will be Tempranillo, Chianti will be Sangiovese, and so on.

WHERE IT COMES FROM

This can be a big area like Bordeaux or Rioja, or a tiny village like Volnay in Burgundy. In Europe it can all get very confusing, and in a country like Italy, even I can't cope with all the new place names they keep coming up with. In the New World, place names are less complicated but as standards rise, particular places are gaining a reputation and are worth looking out for.

For example, in Argentina, Mendoza is the main wine region (all snuggled up against the Andes) but there are some side valleys and higher cooler spots in Mendoza which are better. A Mendoza wine which also mentions Uco or Gualtallary is often better than straight Mendoza, and this is happening right across the New World.

WHAT GRAPE VARIETY?

A lot of wine buffs will try to tell you that the most important factor in the flavour of a wine is the place where the grapes were grown. Well, it may be for 'wine buff wine'. But unless the grape variety is incredibly neutral (and some are), the different flavours of the different varieties are at the heart of the taste of a wine. Everything else flows from the nature of the grape variety.

VARIETAL LABELLING

It may seem weird, but until the New World came barging in, very few wines mentioned their grape variety on the label. So that meant choosing a wine was often like taking a flying leap into a dark pit. With a label full of uninformative terms, often referring to obscure parts of their country of origin and everything in a foreign language, no wonder wine-drinking as a popular pastime, enjoyed by the majority of the population, took so long to take off.

It wasn't until the 1980s that any great attempt to make wine easy to understand took place. Then the Californians and the Australians cut through all the mystifying gobbledegook with one gorgeous, thrilling stroke. If genius is the art of stating the obvious, this was the purest genius of all – just tell everybody what grape variety the wine is made from. Throw away all the stuffy old terms and fanciful titles – just put the name of the grape variety right in the centre of the label.

So simple. All grape varieties taste different. Put the name on the label so that you can tell straight away if it's likely to be a wine you'll enjoy. And if you're beginning to learn about wine from scratch, learning about the different flavours each grape variety has is the easiest and quickest route to wine knowledge and the surest way to make sure you order a wine you like.

WHO MADE IT?

Important. As with everything else in life, some people are better than others. Wine geeks always like small producers best, but big companies can often make good wine when they can be bothered. In general, the name of a person or a company on the label is a better arrow towards good quality than silly, fanciful made-up names that are clearly the result of a marketing man's over-active imagination.

HOW OLD IS IT?

Important. Most wines are best pretty young, and so the most recent year on the label is usually preferable. There are some wines that get better with age – Cabernet Sauvignon often does, Shiraz can, Riesling may. But the flavours do change, and if you're used to young wine flavours – most of us are – you may actually not like the wine so much when it's older, so don't feel any pressure to buy older wine.

OTHER CLUES

Alcoholic strength Important. You want to know how much alcohol you are taking in. But alcoholic strength also affects the style of the wine. Lower alcohol should mean lighter, more ethereal, sometimes not quite dry – but it may also mean thin and sharp. Higher alcohol implies bigger, riper, broader flavours, often chunkier, and sometimes a bit hot at the back of the throat.

Bottle size Usually 75cl or 750ml. You will find a few smaller bottles at 500 or 375ml. You might even see a quarter bottle at 187ml. And there are some magnificent bigger ones at 1500ml and upwards. Many wine lovers say that the 1500ml bottle, or 2-bottle magnum, is the best because the wine matures and mellows best in bottles of this size. And a big bottle always looks fantastic at a party or on the dining table.

Classifications Terms like Riserva/Reserva are sometimes important for wines such as Chianti or Rioja, but often words like Reserve just mean that the wine is bigger, more alcoholic – and more expensive.

Back label A New World habit. It can give you interesting details including how the wine tastes, how oaky it is, which grape varieties were used, how long you can age it for and the best serving temperature. Some retailers also have helpful systems for grading the wine they sell on a scale from bone dry to very sweet for whites, and from light-bodied to full-bodied for reds. Flavour descriptions are often more complete marketing guff. Advice from the person selling you the wine or social media comment is a lot more useful.

CLASSIFICATIONS AND WHERE THEY COME FROM

Try as they might, official classification systems on the label don't help much with indicating the quality of the wine, but here are a few key ones you might come across. All the European systems are based to some extent on the place of origin.

France The basic category is Vin de France (covering basic and more experimental wines). IGP is the next level up, referring to wines from a specific area, followed by AOP (Appellation d'Origine Protégée) or AOC (Appellation d'Origine Contrôlée).

Italy The basic category is Vino (covering basic and more experimental wines). IGP is the next level up, followed by DOP (Denominazione di Origine Protetta), divided into two categories – DOC and DOCG, the highest level.

Spain The basic category is Vino (covering basic and more experimental wines). IGP is the next level up, followed by DOP (Denominación de Origen Protegida). DOCa (Denominación de Origen Calificada) is a super-category for two wines only – Rioja and Priorat.

Apart from my name, this is a typical French-style wine label: strong on provenance, not strong on grape variety, so how do I know what it is going to taste like?

CLARKEY

2018
NEW DAWN
SHIRAZ

SOUTH AUSTRALIA

14% VOL, WINE OF AUSTRALIA, 750ml.

The objective here is to show the simplicity of a typical New World label, led by the grape variety. I can almost taste the wine already.

Portugal The basic category is Vinho (covering both basic wines and more experimental wines). IGP is the next level up, followed by DOP (Denominação de Origem Protegida).

Germany The classification system is based on the ripeness of the grapes and their potential alcohol level. Deutscher Wein is the most basic term, followed by Landwein. QbA is quality wine from one of 13 regions. QmP is the top level, with 6 ascending levels according to ripeness (Kabinett, Spätlese, Auslese, Beerenauslese, Eiswein and Trockenbeerenauslese).

Austria Similar categories to Germany. A newer system based on geographical appellations with stylistic constraints is called DAC but it is totally confusing as there are different rules and regulations for each one. I love Austrian wine but I don't take much notice of this classification system.

United States The AVA (American Viticultural Area) system does not guarantee a quality standard, but merely requires that 85% of grapes in a wine come from the specified AVA. AVAs come in all shapes and sizes and new ones are added every year.

Outside Europe Most countries have something along the lines of the US AVA (American Viticultural Area) system. It guarantees the geographical origin of the wine, but carries no quality connotation.

DRY, MEDIUM OR SWEET?

It would be helpful if the label told you how sweet the wine is but it is not as simple as that. For wines from all countries except Germany, you can generally assume that the wine is dry unless otherwise stated (use the clues below). With global warming, and a general trend towards very ripe flavours – especially in the USA – you might think that quite a lot of the wines you taste, for instance, Sauvignon Blanc and Chardonnay, are not quite dry. And you'd be right. Throughout the world many fairly sweet wines are made from late-harvested (therefore very ripe), but not botrytis-infected grapes.

France You can encounter the following terms for wines: **Brut** is a sparkling wine term for very dry; **Sec** is a sparkling wine term for fairly dry; **Demi-sec** is a sparkling wine term for slightly sweet. **Doux**

or **moelleux** is sweet and **liquoreux** is very sweet. Be aware that wines from appellations that apply specifically to sweet wines, such as Sauternes, make no mention on the label of the fact that the wine is sweet. The most common appellations for sweet wines are: (Alsace) Sélection de Grains Nobles (Alsace wines are currently involved in a bit of a rumpus because a lot of them are quite sweet yet don't say so on the label); (Bordeaux) Barsac, Cadillac, Cérons, Loupiac, Premières Côtes de Bordeaux, Ste-Croix-du-Mont and Sauternes (world-famous Château d'Yquem comes from here); (Loire Valley) Bonnezeaux, Coteaux du Layon, Montlouis-sur-Loire, Quarts de Chaume and Vouvray; (southern Rhône and Languedoc-Roussillon) Muscats; and (South-West) Gaillac, Jurançon, Pacherenc du Vic Bilh (these three can be both sweet and dry), Monbazillac and Saussignac.

Italy Secco is dry; **semisecco** is medium-dry; **abboccato** or **amabile** is medium-sweet; and **dolce** is sweet. Sweet wines include Orvieto, Moscato d'Asti, Moscato di Pantelleria and Vin Santo.

Spain Seco is dry; **semi-seco** is medium; **dulce** is sweet. Sweet wines include Moscatel de Valencia and Pedro Ximénez (PX) sherry.

Germany Wines tend to be at least slightly sweet unless otherwise stated. Germany also has a great sweet wine tradition: when conditions are right, the Riesling grape manages to combine high acidity with stratospheric sugar levels. These wines are normally labelled Beerenauslese (BA) or Trockenbeerenauslese (TBA). The terms **Kabinett**, **Spätlese**, **Auslese**, **Beerenauslese**, **Eiswein** (rare) and **Trockenbeerenauslese** refer to ascending levels of sweetness. **Trocken** is dry and **halbtrocken** or **Feinherb** is off-dry.

Austria Dry wines are more common here than in Germany, but with a warmer climate, they are also a little fuller and riper. Austria makes similar, though weightier, styles to Germany's great sweet Beerenauslese and Trockenbeerenauslese wines. Austrian sweet styles are, in ascending order of sweetness: **Spätlese**, **Auslese**, **Beerenauslese**, **Ausbruch**, **Trockenbeerenauslese** and **Eiswein**.

Hungary **Tokaji** is the classic sweet wine, often made from grapes with botrytis or noble rot. It possesses a remarkable blend of honey, pineapple and barleysugar sweetness with a fairly rip-roaring acidity.

Canada Canada has made a speciality of extremely sweet Icewine (both still and sparkling) using Riesling, Vidal, Cabernet Franc and other varietals. China and Sweden have also released Icewine.

WINE COMPETITIONS AND MEDALS

You often see these awards splashed over labels, but it all depends if the wine competition itself is any good. There are a number of proper wine competitions which are not tied up with producers within any country whose medals you can take seriously. Northern Europe has several, and the two leading British competitions – the International Wine Challenge and the Decanter World Wine Awards – are judged by impartial experts. Their trophies, medals and recommendations are worth following.

However, there are other European wine competitions which seem to spew out double golds, platinums, double platinums and whatever other metal is the world's most valuable at the moment. I'd take those monuments to hyperbole with a fairly large pinch of salt.

There are also national competitions, and regional competitions, solely for the wines of their country or those regions. Some will be a bit too liberal in their awards – home team judging, it's called. But the New World competitions, in particular, are usually judged by a majority of winemakers, rather than wine merchants and wine critics, and can generally be taken seriously.

TRENDY NAMES ON THE LABEL

This is a selection of reasonably hip wine names. Some of these regions make wines like the ancients did 8000 years ago and some of them produce flavours that are totally original and new. And remember that trendiness always up the price.

Argentina	*South Australia*
Buenos Aires	Adelaide Hills (Basket Range
Uco Valley (Tupungato and	and Forest Range)
Gualtallary)	Eden Valley
	Fleurieu Peninsula
Australia	Limestone Coast
Western Australia	
Great Southern	*Victoria*
Manjimup	Beechworth
Pemberton	Gippsland

Heathcote
Macedon Ranges
Mornington Peninsula

New South Wales
Canberra District
New England Highlands
Orange
Tumburumba

Tasmania
Coal River
East Coast
Huon Valley

Brazil
Planalto Catarinense
Serra do Sudeste

Chile
Aconcagua Costa
Bío Bío
Cauquenes
Itata Valley

France
Beaujolais (domaine wines)
Champagne (growers' wines)
Jura
Limoux
Pic St-Loup

Georgia and Armenia

Italy
Alto Adige (whites)
Campania (whites)
Etna in Sicily (reds and whites)

New Zealand
Awatere (Kekerengu)

Bannockburn
Gimblett Gravels
Waiheke Island
Waitaki

Portugal
Dão
Douro
Minho

South Africa
Elgin
Elim
Hemel-en-Aarde
Overberg
Swartland

Spain
Bierzo
Emporda
Manchuela
Rías Baixas
Ribeiro (whites)
Toro
Txakoli/Chacolí
Valdeorras

United States of America
California (Sonoma Coast,
   Anderson Valley, Santa
   Rita Hills)
Maryland
Michigan
New York State (Hudson River)
Oregon (Eola, Amity Hills)
Virginia (Shenandoah Valley)
Washington State (Walla Walla)

Uruguay
Maldonado

WHAT THE BOTTLE TELLS YOU

In the traditional wine world there were a few bottle shapes and glass colours that told you where some wines come from.

Red Bordeaux A high-shouldered bottle made of dark green glass. Used for the tougher red wines, especially those made from the Bordeaux family of grapes – Cabernet Sauvignon, Merlot and Malbec. Most Spanish and Tuscan reds use this shape. Sauvignon Blanc comes in both Bordeaux and Burgundy shapes.

Burgundy A low-shouldered bottle made from pale green glass. Nearly all red Pinot Noir and most white Chardonnay use this shape as do most Syrah and Shiraz reds and most wines from southern French grapes such as red Grenache, Cinsaut and Carignan and white Viognier.

Champagne Similar to Burgundy bottles in shape, but much heavier and generally in darker glass. Decent sparkling wines will be in these bottles too.

German wine A tall, slender bottle, with brown glass for the Rhine and green for the Mosel. Also used in Alsace in France and for Rieslings from around the world.

Bordeaux and Burgundy bottles haven't really changed over time. Nor have most Champagne bottles, although you can find some fairly bizarre shapes from the more self-important producers. Germany is much less strict about colour and shape. There are a few other traditional shapes also – Chianti can still be found in straw-covered flasks in tourist shops or in very old-fashioned neighbourhood *trattorie*. Many of the aromatic grapes such as Muscat, Austria's Grüner Veltliner, Spain's Albariño or Italy's Falanghina and Fiano could be in any shape of bottle.

1 Red Bordeaux 2 Burgundy 3 Champagne and most sparkling wines 4 Tall Germanic flute 5 Port and other fortified wines 6 Provençal rosé 7 Icewine

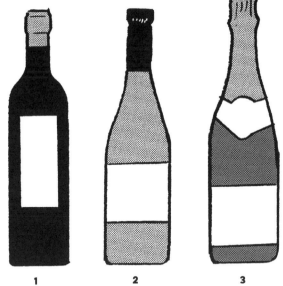

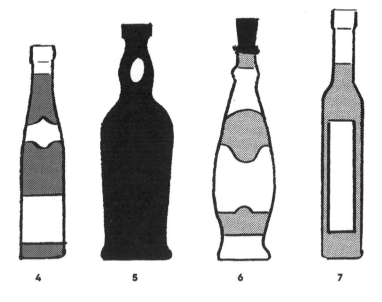

THE CANNY WINE BUYER

One of the joys of being a wine enthusiast today is that we have a wider choice of wine-buying methods than ever before. However much wine I accumulate, it's never going to stop me dropping into my local wine shop to browse, have a chat and pick up a bottle for the evening. This is the way we buy most of our wine nowadays, not by the case, not for laying down, but just as part of our daily shopping.

THE BASIC APPROACH

If you're in a wine region, buy the local wine. So if you usually drink Merlot, but you're in a region where they don't grow Merlot, well, don't ask for it. Ask for what they *do* grow. If you're buying wine in your usual store or supermarket, that's different. You like Merlot – they'll have some. You could just go on drinking the same Merlot forever. Some people drive the same car for years and don't feel the need for a change. But you're missing out because the pleasure you get from drinking wine is a bit more nuanced than the pleasure derived from your daily commute.

But you don't have to do anything very brave. Try this. If you normally drink Chilean Merlot, for instance, next time choose a Merlot from a different country – South Africa, southern France, Argentina or Croatia. The flavours will be different, subtly or considerably, but the general Merlot style that you like will still be there. If you usually like fairly cheap examples from one country, try the fairly cheap examples from the other countries. You don't *have* to trade up.

Trading up If you do want to trade up, start by trading up in the same grape from the country you're used to – i.e. Merlot from Chile – and see if that gives you a buzz. And then think about trading up in other countries' Merlots. And you can apply this strategy to the main red and white grapes quite easily.

Country by country You can also try another strategy – a country by country approach if you like Italian or Spanish or Greek or Argentinian wines – stay with the country but move to different grape varieties and areas. So if you usually drink Argentinian Malbec, well, move across to Argentinian Cabernet Sauvignon or Merlot or Bonarda or Shiraz. You are still in Argentina and these still are wines with that warm, round, friendly Argentinian personality, but definitely different flavours. And suddenly your range of pleasure in wine has got a whole lot wider.

WAYS OF BUYING WINE

Supermarkets and others In many countries these dominate our wine-buying habits. But they are less dominant than they used to be. And many of them have smaller ranges than they used to. Even so, the quality of what supermarkets have is generally higher than it was a generation ago. In particular, the quality of own-label wines remains surprisingly good despite the relentless increase in the costs of production, distribution – and, of course, taxes.

Discounters These are a relatively recent phenomenon, though they have been at work in Europe for years. Prices are always low, sometimes very low, and, given that, most wines are of remarkably good quality. Particularly worth looking out for are their 'specials' when they buy a parcel of wines – and when it's gone it's gone.

Independent merchants There are fewer independent merchants than there used to be, but the quality keeps going up. Usually independents operate out of shops and you can quickly develop a relationship/ friendship with the owner or manager, who is more likely to have bottles open to taste – if they like you. Some independents are online only. Some are very specialized in quite esoteric stuff, and if you are after some rare concoction, these geeky independent wine enthusiasts are the people to call.

Online Online is not so important in wine buying as in many other areas. Perhaps it's because wine is fundamentally a social thing and buying it is quite social, too. Even so, you can use the internet for just about every facet of wine – knowledge, opinion, criticism, peer to peer chat, price comparison and, of course, buying. If you are a keen onliner, things get exponentially better every year – from big supermarkets to the tiniest independent merchant, online is all-pervasive. Options range from wineries to retail wine merchants to specialist online businesses to supermarkets and entrepreneurial brokers who tout for business by joining in internet chat forums.

Wine clubs Most countries have several very good ones with a wide range of wines at every price level. The good thing about wine clubs and societies is that they have loads of activities – tastings, talks, dinners and trips – that's sort of what clubs do – and so you can enjoy yourself, learn, and buy, all at the same time.

Cheap own-label wines These *can* be good in a decent discounter or supermarket because most years there will be wine left in a producer's vats which needs to be cleared and the big retailers can buy it often for the cost of clearing the vats. You'll just have to buy examples of whatever of these 'everyday low price' wines you can find – and whichever one you like most, buy that. The flavours may chop and change during the year as different vats need emptying or different suppliers need to ease their cashflow, so you'll just have to take advantage whenever the cheapo tastes good to you.

On holiday/direct from the producer Logically buying direct from a local producer should be the cheapest way of buying wine. Well … be careful. If you're determined to load the car with the local co-op's wine that tasted fantastic by a campfire in the pine-scented glade near the Med where you pitched your tent, well, you'll save lots of money. But don't expect it to taste the same when you're back in your normal urban milieu. It won't. It'll almost always taste worse. Though, I don't know, even if it does taste worse but can bring back happy holiday memories, well, I guess that's worth it. Just don't be surprised when your friends who *weren't* on holiday with you don't think much of it.

Some châteaux and wineries are only too happy to sell wine from the cellar door or by mail order. For some, it's the only way they sell it. If you're visiting, call first to check opening times and if necessary to make an appointment. But beware: even in this age of online shopping you can still run up against archaic trade barriers. Wherever you live you'll generally have to pay a customs duty on wine shipped to you from abroad. And in some US states it is actually illegal for consumers to buy wine direct from outside the state. The top Bordeaux châteaux and the better domaines in, say, Burgundy will receive visitors, sometimes only with advance warning, but will rarely sell you wine. The commercial structure of importer-wholesaler-retailer/restaurateur-consumer generally works in the interest of all concerned, even the final consumer.

When you buy wine direct from a producer, being able to make a choice from wines tasted at the place where they are made compensates you for the expense of getting there and back and getting the wines home, too.

Auction houses Auction rooms are ideal for anyone wanting to buy a large range of the most prestigious wines from older vintages that are difficult to find anywhere else. A wine sale catalogue from a top auction house will have wine enthusiasts drooling over wine names they certainly don't see in their local wine shop every day. The larger houses (Christie's, Sotheby's and Bonhams in London and Acker, Merrall & Condit and Zachys in the USA) hold auctions around the world, including in Japan and Hong Kong. Top auction houses make a considerable effort today to check the provenance of their wines. If you have never bought wine at an auction before, a good place to start is at a local auctioneer rather than at the famous international houses. Online auctions are also popular and have similar pros and cons to live auctions.

En primeur This is a top-end activity where you buy smart wines when they are still usually in barrel. Bordeaux and Burgundy are the two biggest players. Supposedly, you'll save lots of money and get first dibs at stuff you'll never be able to buy again, or stuff which will cost twice as much in a few years' time. Well, it used to be like that. But en primeur wines are now so expensive that only the very special wines get ever more valuable in a few years. And, I don't know, I don't get that much pleasure from drinking a wine I'm convinced I've paid too much for in the first place.

Brokers The world demand for fine wine has created the role of the wine broker. These are for the really keen wine enthusiast. Brokers hold stock whereas auction houses don't. And there are plenty of brokers out there. Anyone wanting to find a particular wine from a particular vintage should deal with the brokers, some of whom are seriously large operations with bases in London, New York and/or Hong Kong.

ARE THERE BARGAINS OUT THERE?

Definitely, yes. But you may have to go outside your comfort zone. If an area is popular, demand is high, and so there's no great pressure to make the wines cheaper. If the wine is popular and there's not much of it made, then there's no incentive to lower the price, and if you see what looks like a bargain, it's unlikely to be much good.

In the most expensive areas – Burgundy in France is a good example – there are the popular villages where the wines will have scary prices and, frankly, unless you're a Burgundy freak you don't need to go there. Yet there are more obscure villages which struggle to sell their wines and where the flavours are good and the prices almost reasonable. In well-known areas go off the beaten track.

The best way to find bargains is to go to unpopular, less well-known places (see page 106). These places may be obscure because the wine isn't very nice, but most places in Europe and the New World have a fairly good level of quality nowadays, and some perfectly good places just haven't been noticed yet. Buying these wines before they become famous will be your best chance of a bargain.

One of the worst ways to try to get a bargain is to believe the banners proclaiming Buy One Get One Free (often called BOGOF), or half price or 50% off. Heavily discounted wines are rarely worth more than their discounted prices. Sometimes their names are completely made up. Sometimes they are big brands desperate for market share at any price.

Bizarrely, at Christmas and other holiday periods, the big supermarkets and discounters slash the prices of the most glamorous luxury wine of all – Champagne. Well-known quality Champagne brands are often reduced by 30% or more, so keep a look out. And made-up Champagne names appear for the same price as a bottle of Prosecco which, to my amazement, are often quite good. (Global warming has affected the Champagne region in north-east France more than most places, so there's a lot more tolerably ripe wine being made than there used to be.)

When a whole country gets cheaper These discounts cover all of one country's wines and are well worth taking advantage of. You may be able to save 25% on, say, buying Australian or French or New Zealand wines.

Buying more than one bottle These discounts can kick in from as few as two bottles. More often you need to buy six. Combine these with a generic discount or a Champagne promotion, and you can genuinely save money without compromising on quality.

NAVIGATING A WINE LIST

The mark-ups in restaurants and bars are quite enough to take your thirst away. But remember, you are not just paying for the liquid in your glass – it's all the other stuff that makes you happy in a good bar or restaurant.

Head for the 'by the glass' section on the wine list, and use it to try out new stuff. If you don't like the wine for some reason, you only have to get through one glass, not a whole bottle.

Opening a wine list should be a thrill. What delights will I find? What new adventures or old favourites lurk? And will I spot a bargain? Your mouth should be watering as you begin to scroll down the list.

So why is it that even I often feel a sense of nervousness and trepidation when I'm handed the list? Well, confusion is often my first response. And shock at the pricing is often my second response. And, unless you're lucky and get an easy-going, friendly wine waiter (or sommelier, as they're sometimes called), pressure is another problem. I just came out for a bite and a drink with my friends. Why am I feeling so tense?

So. You're not alone. How can we navigate the wine list successfully?

Have an idea of the price you want to pay Don't feel you must pay more than you're happy with to try to impress your friends. And don't let a wine waiter pressure you into buying a more expensive bottle than you can really afford. The wine waiter's job is to make you feel happy, not stressed. If you are going to have two bottles don't blow your budget on the first.

You don't have to be adventurous If you don't know much about wine, you don't have to be adventurous. You can perfectly happily stick with what you know. If you do know a bit about wine, going to a restaurant is a good opportunity to try something new. Often lesser-known wines are a reasonable price. The South of France, Portugal, Spain (apart from Rioja) and Italy (apart from Tuscany and Piedmont) are good hunting grounds. Don't expect to find bargains among the classics like Bordeaux and Burgundy or California's Napa Valley Cabernet Sauvignon. The prices often make me shudder. On an uninspiring list, opt for wines from Australia, New Zealand or South America – they are the most likely to be reliable and good value.

You don't have to talk to the wine waiter if you don't want to. But if you do want some advice, be firm about what price you're prepared to pay – although it's not always easy in front of your friends to say, I only want to spend so much – unless you're all sharing the bill. Don't be bullied by over-assiduous waiters – make sure the bottle is within your reach and top up your glasses when you want to.

If you don't like the wine but there's nothing wrong with it – we've all been there – you can't really send it back. Some friendly staff will get you something else, some won't. There are a couple of faults that you may find (see page 142) – and in these cases don't be nervous about complaining. I say that, but it's easier said than done if you're not sure. I've often enough 'grinned and bore it', only to realize as the bottle is drained that – dammit – there *was* something wrong. Why didn't I complain?

Wine by the glass Don't reject the 'wine by the glass' list. A good restaurant will serve a selection of interesting wines by the glass. This is often my favourite part of the list, because I can experiment for the cost of a glass rather than a full bottle. If there are four of you, order four different glasses. Try each other's wines. See which you like best. It's fun, it's social. And you can then order a whole bottle of your favourite wine to follow.

House wines Don't dismiss the House Red and White on a wine list. Any decent bar or restaurant nowadays will have made an effort to get some attractive, bright, gluggable grog as their basic wine. If it's nice, you can stick with it or move on, that's up to your mood and your pocket. But just remember, in most wine-producing regions of the world, the local house red or white is what most of the locals drink.

Bring your own (BYO) Some restaurants – often Asian ones – will let you bring your own wine and charge you a 'corkage' fee. It's a brilliant system. No more wine list and wine waiter problems. Look out for the BYO sign or a sign that says the restaurant is unlicensed. In that case, they might not even charge you corkage.

WINE FOR ENJOYING ON ITS OWN

The days when wine always had to accompany food are long gone. Some people make a fuss about food and wine matching, but most modern wines are a good drink in their own right – with or without food. I choose lighter, fresher styles if I'm drinking wine on its own.

Red wines Don't go for those great big Shirazes and Cabernets and don't go for high alcohol, heavily oaked monsters – leave them for when the barbecue is already smoking.

The most famous 'drink it alone' red is Beaujolais from France and I start dreaming of a summertime picnic in a sun-dappled riverside meadow as soon as I sniff the stuff. Virtually every country produces some lighter – and cheaper – reds. Italian Bardolinos and Valpolicellas are delightful. Spanish Garnachas, Austrian Zweigelts and the simple Chilean Pinot Noirs and Merlots or Argentinian Malbecs hit the spot, too. The days when cheap red wine was sour and to be avoided are now long gone. Nowadays it's the cheap, young red that is fresh and thirst-quenching.

White wines Almost anything but big, oaky numbers will positively hurtle down your throat. So leave those heavy Chardonnays alone. Stick with Sauvignon Blanc or dry Riesling – or Pinot Grigio if you are not in the mood for anything tasting of much. All the European countries now make fresh, lighter styles. French Gascogne or Muscadet, Spanish Albariño, Portuguese Vinho Verde, Austrian Grüner Veltliner, and loads of Italian styles like Soave, Fiano, Falanghina or Grillo, even Pinot Grigio is sometimes tasty – all these do the trick. Romania or Hungarian Pinot Grigios are tastier and cheaper. As with the reds, buy them young, buy them cheap and drink them quick.

Rosé wines You can always drink pink without food. Or with food. Or with friends. Or without friends. Indoors. Outdoors. Monday, Wednesday, Friday or Sunday. You get the message. Spain probably makes the tastiest dry rosés, but southern France is good, too. Anything not called Côtes de Provence will be cheaper. There are some lovely light Italian ones, too.

SPECIAL OCCASIONS

What *is* a Special Occasion? I'd say it's any day when you are happy, you've got some friends who have smiles on their faces, and someone's getting a nice meal ready. It doesn't have to be a 50th birthday, a wedding anniversary, a celebration of getting your degree or passing your driving test – and the food doesn't have to be rare and expensive. So many people say to me, 'oh, I'm saving this bottle for a Special Occasion'. The occasion never seems to come. And if it does, the poor old bottle is laden with expectation, and hardly ever seems to be as good as you'd hoped. I say to them – next time the postman knocks and he's got a smile on his face – open the bottle. Well, that's a bit extreme, but I bet all of us could find the time to open a special bottle of wine in the next week or two. Most bottles don't need much aging, all they need is for everyone to be in the right mood.

Special wines And if you're determined to celebrate a Special Occasion with some special wine – great. I'm sure your guests will be delighted. But don't trade up wildly to types of wine that you don't know, just because you think they are 'more special'. They're not more special if you don't like them. Many people think they should shell out loadsa money on things like smart Bordeaux or Burgundy from France, or Barolo and Brunello from Italy, when they never normally drink such things. They probably won't enjoy them. Frankly, most top European wines are a bit of an acquired taste and work best with food: you have to work at enjoying them.

Most of the super-expensive prestige cuvée Champagnes don't get my seal of approval. They are fiendishly expensive for what they are and often seem to be drunk by celebs who have more money than sense. Some of the packaging is indeed beautiful – elegant bottles, lots of gold foil and even cellophane wrapping – and obviously this will impress the heck out of your friends. And remember that behind all this surface froth, most of the prestige cuvées from good Champagne houses really are their most rigorous selection of wines from their best vineyards in the finest vintage years, and for that you'll be charged a high price.

So I would suggest that if you want to spoil yourself and your guests, think which styles of wine you like – and then trade up to a better example. If you like Chilean Merlot, trade up to a better one. If you like New Zealand Sauvignon Blanc, trade up to a better one. And if you like Champagne? ... Use the extra money to buy an extra bottle, or a bigger bottle, of the one you like, rather than pay through the nose for a deluxe fancy bottle. Magnums (1500ml or two bottles) always make a great present.

COMPARE AND CONTRAST

Excuse me stating the obvious, but wines do all taste different. Grape varieties have different tastes. Warm countries make wines that are different to cool-country wines. Wines from a valley floor taste different from wines grown on a mountainside. Wines aged in oak barrels taste different from wines aged in stainless steel. Wines made by men with moustaches taste different... well, not quite. But you see what I mean. There's a whole world of different flavours and experiences out there. How are we going to make the best of it if we don't contrast and compare?

The simplest example is grapes. A Sauvignon Blanc makes wine with a sharp, fresh, green-ish flavour. A Chardonnay makes a softer, rounder, fleshier wine that can be quite golden in colour. Completely different. We'll probably prefer one to the other. But if we don't compare them, how will we ever know?

It's the same with countries. Chianti is one of Italy's most famous reds, Rioja is Spain's most famous red, in France Bordeaux and Burgundy make world famous reds. And they're all completely different. If we don't compare, how will we know which one we like best and why? Or let's make it even simpler. New World wines – from places like California, Australia, Chile and Argentina – are riper, softer, lusher than wines made from the same grape varieties in Europe.

And what about age? When we look at a wine selection, some wines will be older, some younger. They'll taste quite different. Do we prefer the exuberant juiciness of youth or the more reflective flavours of age? Gotta compare. Do we like wines bone dry, or fruity, or slightly sweet? Gotta compare. And so it goes on. To get the best out of the wonderful world of wine, don't just stick to one thing, be adventurous, contrast and compare. You'll quickly work out what you like and what you don't.

WHERE TO FIND VALUE (see right)
If somewhere is trendy, if somewhere has the spotlight of fame or fashion shone upon it, and you want value? You need to go somewhere else. Fashion makes prices go up, or quality go down – or both. Don't go there.

WHERE TO FIND VALUE

Argentina
Mendoza (reds)
Neuquén
San Juan

Australia
Great Southern
Langhorne Creek
Limestone Coast
South Australia (state-wide
    blends)

California
Lodi
Monterey
Paso Robles
Santa Maria Valley

Chile
Colchagua
Leyda
Limarí
Maule

Eastern Europe
Greece (white)
Moldova (red and white)
Romania (red and white)

France
Beaujolais-Villages
Languedoc (Corbières)
Loire Valley (Muscadet,
    Sauvignon de Touraine)
Rhône (Côtes du Rhône)
Roussillon

Italy
Campania (white –
    Falanghina, Fiano and
    Greco)
Langhe (red and white)
Marche (white – Verdicchio,
    Pecorino)
Sicily
Veneto (red and white)

New Zealand
Gisborne (whites)

Portugal
Alentejo
Bairrada
Douro
Minho
Tejo
Vinho Verde

South Africa
Breedekloof
Durbanville
Robertson
Wellington

Spain
Calatayud
Campo de Borja
Extremadura
Jerez
Rueda
Somontano

ESSENTIAL KIT

The rituals of opening, serving
and tasting wine are mostly built
on sound reasoning but they are
meaningless if they don't help you to
enjoy yourself and get the best out of
your wine.

FROM MAGNUMS TO CANS

Bigger is better? Well, up to a point, yes. Most wine bottles are 75cl. But imagine a bottle twice the size, 150cl. It's called a magnum. It looks more imposing, more indulgent, but also more generous as it dominates the table. And the experts say that a wine evolves most effectively when it's in a magnum. Certainly the wine ages more slowly. You can get much bigger bottles: 3 litre, 6 litre and so on. Most of the big ones have got biblical names: an 8-litre giant is called a Balthazar, a 12-litre monster is a Melchior. You rarely see anything bigger than a magnum, though Champagne producers do turn out some pretty vast receptacles for publicity purposes, and regions like Bordeaux or Napa Valley in California sometimes can't resist the odd boastful brute.

Of course, your wine doesn't have to be in a bottle at all. Bag in box wines have been around for ages. These employ a collapsible bag inside a cardboard box – or any sort of box, I suppose. They used to be pretty filthy, but modern technology means that if you put a decent wine into the box, you'll get a decent one out. Cans are also used for wine, though nothing particularly tasty has gone into them yet. But there's been an absolute revolution in beer cans. Some of the best beers on the planet are now in cans. Wines are still a long way off. And anyway, what can you do with an empty can? With an empty bag in box, you can blow up the bag and use it as a pillow on the beach.

CLOSURES: FROM CORKS TO SCREWCAPS

What's the best way to seal a bottle of wine? The cork is thought of as the traditional material, and a good cork is indeed very suitable because it expands sideways into the neck of the bottle, creating a very tight fit. Cork was discovered by the Romans – like most things – and for the last three centuries has been unchallenged as the supreme wine bottle closure. Until now.

At the beginning of this century there was an epidemic of contaminated corks which spoilt wine with their dirty, musty smell. (Remember, a cork is merely a lump of bark from a tree that has been moulded into the cork shape.) The reaction to this was the rapid development of the metal screwcap. Previously you would only find screwcaps on cheap wines, but they are excellent, reliable closures, and an increasing number of high-quality whites (and some reds), especially in the New World, now use screwcaps by choice, resulting in much fresher, more consistent, bottles of wine.

There are other closures too. You may find a plastic cork in your bottle. You'll know the cork is plastic because it'll be hell trying to extract the thing from the bottle, and it won't be much easier twisting the cork off your corkscrew.

A few very smart operations use glass stoppers for closures. These work well but I always think they're a bit fiddly. Still, a couple of hundred years ago they would put a layer of oil on top of the wine, soak some rags in oil, wrap them round a lump of wood and cram this lot into the bottle's neck. Anything is an improvement on that.

FROM CRYSTAL TO PAPER CUPS

I used to be one of the 'a tooth mug will do' brigade. And I have drunk stunning wine out of a tooth mug (Sassicaia 1968) and a plastic mug (Margaux 1961). They were fantastic. I can still vividly recall the flavours. Or was it the occasion I'm recalling (my bedroom for the Sassicaia, and a car park in the Rhône Valley for the Margaux)? I think that's quite enough detail, thank you. And the only time I used to draw the line was with paper cups. Particularly the BBC's paper cups. Absolutely everything, from tap water to tea to vintage Champagne tastes like a BBC paper cup when drunk from a BBC paper cup.

Nowadays, I'm a believer in good glasses. They *do* make a difference to how a wine tastes. The shape and the size – even the thickness – of a glass affects the wine's flavour. Don't ask me how. I've read all the science put out by glassmakers like Riedel and Zalto and can't understand why you need a different shape and size of glass for virtually every different grape variety on earth – unless, of course, it's that they make oodles more money that way. But without a doubt a bigger glass, preferably with a reasonably chubby bowl, and one which narrows a bit at the top to catch the wine's perfume, does give you more pleasure. Some of that will be because wines nearly always improve with aeration – whenever you see wine buffs, they're always swirling the wine round in their glasses. And some of that will be because you feel more pampered with a big glass, the wine does look better, you look better with a big glass and, for that matter, the world looks better through a big glass.

Good glasses do make a difference to how a wine tastes and the ideal glass for red and white wine is a fairly large tulip shape. **1** A decent fat bowl is best for red wine. **2** A smaller version works well for white wine. **3** A stemless tumbler and French bistro glass are practical alternatives. **4** A copita or nosing glass is good for fortified wines. **5** Fizz prefers a tall, slender glass as this helps the bubbles to last longer.

SERVING WINE

If you want to taste wine at its best,
to enjoy all its flavours and aromas,
to admire its colours and texture,
it's worth following a few simple
procedures.

SERVING TEMPERATURES

There are no hard and fast rules here. If I had to generalize I'd say too cold is better than too warm, because it's easy to warm a glass of wine up by cupping it in your hands. If you're not doing anything physically demanding, you can clasp the bottle between your thighs for a bit.

Quick trick Cooling wine down involves fridges or ice buckets. If you do need to cool stuff down quickly, fill an ice bucket with ice *and* water – *and* a handful of salt. This works really quickly.

White and rosé wines With white or pink wines, and with fizz, to be honest you can leave them in the fridge all day, and they'll come out nice and cold. Just remember, the colder the wine, the less flavour it has, so some whites, like white Burgundy or an oaked Chardonnay, taste better not quite so cold – say with just a couple of hours in the chiller. Mature wines – and that includes good fizz – may also only want a couple of hours' cooling down. Young snappy whites, like Sauvignon Blanc or Riesling, are at their most refreshing really pretty cool – their acidity will be more marked, and their flavour less intense, but that's fine. The same with fizz. Really cold fizz crackles and sparkles on your tongue more vividly than merely cool fizz, where you'll get more flavour, but less fun from the bubbles.

Red wines If you let red wine get too warm, it can seem to fall apart, and in a way, that *is* what's happening – the alcohol, the fruit, the acid and tannin all seem to head off in different directions. If you cool a hot red wine down in a rush, the wine may still taste disappointing. People talk about serving red wines at room temperature – but just remember, the old timers made these rules long before anyone had central heating. Room temperature in winter might have been positively glacial. Again, slightly cool is better than slightly warm, because unless you are eating in an igloo, the wine will naturally warm up in the glass.

Some young reds are often served chilled – Beaujolais is one example, Valpolicella is another, Rioja *joven* (i.e. young and not oaked) is another. That can work pretty well in summer. But don't overchill them, because red wine that is too cold loses all its fruit, and even a good wine can taste hard and raw. But two points: don't warm red up by a fire or on a radiator – it'll taste like fruit stew. And don't put it in the microwave. Be patient. Cup it in your hand.

WARM *Over 20°C (68°F)*
No wine tastes good above a comfortable room
temperature of about 20°C (68°F)

ROOM TEMPERATURE *15° to 20°C (59° to 68°F)*
Chewy and blackcurranty reds
Warm and spicy reds
Warming, fortified wines (e.g port and sweet Madeira)

COOL ROOM TEMPERATURE *13° to 15°C (55° to 59°F)*
Silky, strawberryish reds

COOL *11° to 13°C (52° to 55°F)*
Light and juicy reds
Tangy fortified wines (e.g. oloroso sherry and dry Madeira)
Golden sweet wines

COLD *8° to 11°C (46° to 52°F)*
Intense, nutty whites
Ripe, toasty whites
Aromatic whites
Gutsy rosés
Vintage Champagne

CHILLED *6° to 8°C (43° to 46°F)*
Green, tangy whites
Sparkling wines
Delicate rosés
Lightest tangy fortifieds (e.g. fino sherry)

WELL CHILLED *4° to 6°C (40° to 43°F)*
Bone-dry neutral whites
Sweet rosés
Cheap sparkling wines

OPENING THE BOTTLE

Dead simple. Twist the screwcap. Remove. Pour. Luckily for us, a lot of wine really is that simple nowadays. But if there's a cork in the bottle neck – well, here's how.

Corkscrew Keep it simple. The waiter's friend is a compact corkscrew that can fit into your pocket. It's all you need. This corkscrew also has a hinged lever which allows you to coax the cork out without having to put the bottle between your legs and give it a mighty tug.

There's usually some metal foil over the top of the bottle. You can easily rip this off using the point of the corkscrew's spiral bit. Some corkscrews also have a little knife attached. You can use this to cut the foil more daintily if you want. So the foil's off. Put the bottle on a flat surface.

Insert the spiral into the middle of the cork. Twist it until the point begins to emerge from the cork. Then either heave the cork out with brute force or apply the lever to the lip of the bottle and ease the cork out. And if that's all a bit much, next time buy wine in a screwcap bottle, or one in a box, or a can.

ALL THAT AIR: TO DECANT OR NOT?

I admit it, I used to be one of those deniers who said, no, that decanting stuff is all old hat. Modern wines don't need to be opened in advance, don't need to 'breathe' – just crack the bottle open and pour. It'll be fine.

Well, I was wrong. Certainly you *can* just crack a modern bottle open and pour – the wine will be fine. But contact with air massively increases the flavour of wine – and in particular those modern wines with their clickety-click screwcaps. These wines – and they include most of the Sauvignons, Chardonnays, Pinot Grigios and Pinot Noirs that we're likely to drink – are nowadays made in a very precise, oxygen-free way. This is to avoid any hint of infections or decay in the wine. But one result of this is that the wines wear a sort of straitjacket because you have to let some oxygen into wine to help it develop flavour and perfume.

That's why the second glass from a screwcap bottle is always better than the first glass. Screwcaps are so good at keeping air out of a bottle that when you twist and pour, the wine is positively shocked into life by the contact with the air. Indeed, when I open screwcaps, I often pour a little wine out, put the screwcap back on, and give the bottle a shake. If that sounds sacrilegious – hey, we're just talking about a bottle of wine here. It really does wake up the flavours.

If you want to 'decant' a wine, use a decanter if you've got one, otherwise a glass or china jug will be fine. As a general rule, older wines need less oxygen – they're a bit more fragile – so don't 'decant' them for too long. And if people tell you it's only red wines that need decanting – that's not true either. White wines look amazing in a decanter – deep, golden and lush. The only problem here is keeping the wine cold – your decanter may not fit that easily into a fridge or an ice bucket. And anyway, we usually drink white wines faster than red, and talk about them less, so opening the bottle and giving it a shake will probably be fine for most whites. Don't shake the old ones; anything – or anyone – old prefers gentle treatment.

OPENING A BOTTLE OF FIZZ

You don't want the wine to cascade out and cover the wall, the table and your guests with a flood of foam. So here are a few tips:

Make sure the bottle is cold Chill it right down. Warm fizz is much more likely to explode out of the bottle and cover everyone with foam.

Don't aim the bottle at anybody Even in fun. A fizz cork can come out so fast you could blind somebody. I mean it. It happens every year.

Remove the foil Whichever way you like.

Now for the action Put your hand, or at very least your thumb, over the cork and its wire cage, and unwind the wire. If you feel *any* pressure under your hand, don't take the cage off – remove cork and cage in the same movement. Otherwise, take the wire cage off carefully. Immediately put your thumb or hand back on the cork, then try to twist the cork and the bottle in opposite directions. Finally, I often end up just twisting the cork. Wine buffs say you should twist the bottle. Yes, in a perfect world…

Pouring You don't want the wine to foam all over the place. So: tilt the glass (ideally a tall flute one) and pour slowly on to the tilted side. If you've got a lot of glasses to fill, put a splash of wine in the bottom of each glass, then you can fill the glasses later and they're much less likely to froth over. But if they do, hey, fizz is about fun, not about etiquette. If you make a mess, well your guests will probably laugh themselves silly. It's actually not a bad way to get a party going with a bang.

MATCHING WINE AND FOOD

Modern wine mostly tastes pretty good to excellent by itself. It doesn't need food as an accompaniment as wine did in the past. Old-fashioned wines often did because they were acid or bitter and lacked fruit. Preserving and enhancing the fruit flavour in a wine is one of the hallmarks of the New Age of wine we all live in. And drinking wine for the sheer pleasure of its flavour is a recent phenomenon in most wine-producing countries.

Take a look at the food we eat, too. Anyone living in a big city could eat a different regional or national cuisine every day for a month, many of them from places where wine played no part in the traditional mealtime experience. So the old rules of what wine goes with what food can't really be applied. But they don't have to be. That very drinkability of most modern wine means it will taste pretty good with most food. In simple terms, if you drink the wine you're in the mood for and eat the food you're in the mood for, it'll probably work – so long as you're eating and drinking with the friends that you're in the mood for. OK. If you're really serious about matching food and wine, people have written whole books on the subject. If you're not too bothered – and, frankly, most of the time I'm not – well, here are a few tips:

Local wine with local food If you're in a wine-producing region, drink the local wine with the local food. Sometimes they've been going together for a thousand years.

Making wine the main event If you want to focus on the wine as the main event, keep the food simple. Red meat with red, and white fish with white sounds pretty dull, but it can be magic.

Red wine, white wine Talking of red wine/red meat, white wine/white fish or fowl, it does work. It is best like that. But you can drink red with fish – preferably a soft red – and you can drink full-flavoured, dry whites with beef and lamb. I've been to dinners where they've served Champagne or sweet Sauternes or vintage port with red meat. All weirdly stunning combinations. Or was it just the company? Was I having too much fun? And that's a bad thing?

Rosé Dry and fruity rosés make excellent partners for a whole range of dishes, from delicate fish to rich, spicy food, but steer away from heavy meat dishes.

Light and heavy It's easy to say light wines with light food, heavy wines with heavy food. Maybe, in a perfect world. Pasta and pizza can get pretty heavy, but light, fresh, edgy reds often go best. The local wine in Bologna (where spaghetti ragù comes from) is bright, frothy Lambrusco, for goodness' sake. Burgundy has some of the richest food in the world, and some of the most delicate, nuanced wines. They seem to think it works.

Dry sparkling wines These are good all-rounders, and are particularly good with shellfish and smoked fish. Champagne with oysters is a classic luxury match, although non-vintage Champagne is more suitable than richer, more expensive vintage ones.

Fortified wines Tangy ones go well with nibbles such as olives and salted almonds, and many tapas dishes. Smoked fish is good, too. Warming ones suit many cheeses and also chocolate.

Rich sweet wines These work well with blue cheeses and sweet food.

Cheese Cheese works with red wine because it softens and flattens the wine's flavour, so a cheap red wine is probably just as good as a pricey one. So don't waste your best red on the cheese board. You could try white. White goes really well with most cheeses.

Chocolate Chocolate blasts the flavour of a wine, but many wines are chastened and changed by the combination. And I'm talking full-bodied dry reds here. Wines like sweet port or rich old sherries are always worth a punt with chocolate.

Curry and wine They say curry kills wine. Well, yes and no. Chilli definitely strips a lot of the taste from wine and tough red wines just end up tougher, but soft reds aren't bad, and good Pinot Noir and red Burgundy are really very good. But would you really pair an expensive Burgundy with a curry? Cheaper Pinot Noir is rather good, so is Valpolicella, and Beaujolais isn't bad. But I prefer white, preferably zesty, snappy Sauvignon Blanc.

Fish and chips Fantastic with Champagne. If you're in that sort of mood, anything goes fantastic with Champagne.

Vinegar They say you can't drink wine with vinegary foods because vinegar is usually made from sour wine. Actually, you can. Vinegar will make most white wines taste richer and sweeter.

Tricky matches do exist There are one or two things whose flavour simply doesn't seem to work with wine. Globe artichokes leave wine tasting of metal and oily fish like mackerel make wine taste metallic, though you might give dry sherry a go. Oysters – I know they say oysters go well with Champagne or Chablis. Whatever you drink with oysters tastes of zinc.

MATCHING FOOD AND WINE

In many cases the local food and wine combinations that have developed over the years simply cannot be bettered. And sometimes it can be a good idea to let the wine dictate the choice of food – with very special bottles, when you have found an irresistible bargain or when you are casting around for culinary inspiration. Here are a few ideas to get you started on being more adventurous.

Cabernet Sauvignon All over the world Cabernet Sauvignon makes full-flavoured, reliable red: the ideal food wine. It seems to have a particular affinity with lamb, but partners all plain roast or grilled meats and game as well as many sauced meat dishes such as beef casserole, steak and kidney pie or dishes with mushrooms.

Chardonnay More than almost any other grape, Chardonnay responds to different climatic conditions and to the winemaker's art. This, plus the relative ease with which it can be grown, accounts for the marked gradation of flavours and styles: from steely, cool-climate austerity to almost tropical lusciousness. The relatively sharp end of the spectrum is one of the best choices for simple fish dishes; most Chardonnays are superb with roast chicken or other white meat; the really full, rich, New World-style blockbusters need rich fish and seafood dishes. Oaky Chardonnays go well with smoked fish.

Gamay The grape of red Beaujolais, Gamay is particularly good lightly chilled on hot summer days. Its acidity provides a satisfying foil to the richness of meat dishes and it's also a good choice for many vegetarian dishes.

Grenache/Garnacha Frequently blended with other grapes, Grenache nonetheless dominates, with its high alcoholic strength and rich, spicy flavours. These are wines readily matched with food: barbecues and casseroles for heavier wines; almost anything for lighter reds and rosés – vegetarian dishes, charcuterie, picnics, grills, and even meaty fish such as tuna and salmon.

Merlot Merlot makes soft, rounded, fruity wines that are some of the easiest red wines to enjoy without food, yet are also a good choice with many kinds of food – spicier game dishes, herby terrines and pâtés, pheasant, pigeon, duck or goose; substantial casseroles made with wine; and the soft fruitiness of Merlot is perfect for pork, liver, turkey, and savoury foods with a hint of sweetness such as Iberico or Parma ham.

Pinot Noir The great grape of Burgundy has taken its food-friendly complexity all over the wine world. However, nothing can beat the marriage of great wine with sublime local food that is Burgundy's heritage, and Burgundian dishes make perfect partners for Pinot Noir: coq au vin, boeuf bourguignon, rabbit with mustard, braised ham, chicken with tarragon, entrecôtes from prized Charolais cattle with a rich red-wine sauce … the list is endless. Pinot Noir's subtle flavours make it a natural choice for complex meat dishes, but it is excellent with plain grills and roasts. New World Pinots are often richer and fruitier – good with grills and roasts and a match for salmon or tuna. The best Pinot Noir red wines are wasted on cheese.

Riesling Good dry Rieslings are excellent with spicy cuisine. Sweet Rieslings are best enjoyed for their own lusciousness but are suitable partners to fruit-based desserts. In between, those with a fresh acid bite and some residual sweetness can counteract the richness of, say, goose or duck, and the fuller examples can be good with Asian food and otherwise hard-to-match salads.

Sauvignon Blanc Tangy green flavours and high acidity are the hallmarks of this grape. Led by New Zealand, New World Sauvignons are some of the snappiest, tastiest whites around and make good, thirst-quenching aperitifs. Brilliant with seafood and Asian cuisine, they also go well with tomato dishes, salads and goats' cheese.

Sémillon Dry white Bordeaux is excellent with fish and shellfish; fuller, riper New World Semillons are equal to spicy food and rich sauces, often going even better with meat than with fish; sweet Sémillons can partner many puddings, especially rich, creamy ones. Sémillon also goes well with many cheeses, and Sauternes with Roquefort is a classic combination.

Syrah/Shiraz Modern Syrah or Shiraz can be rich and exotic or scented and savoury, but it always offers loads of flavour and is superb with full-flavoured food. It is the classic barbecue wine, also brilliant with roasts, game, hearty casseroles, charcuterie and tangy cheeses.

Tempranillo Spain's best native red grape makes juicy wines for drinking young, and matures well in a rich (usually) oaky style. Good with game, cured hams and sausages, casseroles and meat grilled with herbs, particularly roast lamb.

Zinfandel California's much-planted, most versatile grape is used for a bewildering variety of wine styles from bland, sweetish pinks to rich, succulent, fruity reds. And the good red Zinfandels themselves vary greatly in style, from relatively soft and light to big and beefy, but they're always ripe and ready for spicy, smoky, unsubtle food: barbecued meat, haunches of lamb, venison or beef, game casseroles, sausages, Tex-Mex, the Beach Boys, The Eagles – anything rowdy – Zin copes with them all.

LEFTOVER WINE
Leftover white wine keeps better than red. The extra acid freshens whites, while reds often lose their fruit after a day or so. Even so, any wine, red or white, keeps better in the fridge than in a warm kitchen. And most wines, if well made in the first place, will be perfectly fine, if not pristine, after two or three days re-corked in the fridge. Young, screwcapped wines, especially whites, might even improve and can easily last a week and still be good to drink. A variety of gadgets are sold to keep wine fresh in an opened bottle. The ones that work by blanketing the wine with heavier-than-air inert gas are much better than those that create a vacuum in the air space in the bottle.

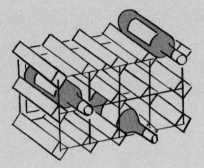

KEEPING WINE

This section may not be relevant to
most of us. Statistics tell us that most
wine is consumed within 24 hours
of being bought, but just in case you
are one of those who gets the wine
collecting bug, or if you just find
you often have more wine sitting
around than you expected (just tell
your friends: that'll sort it) – here are
some tips.

AT HOME

I first started storing wine under my bed at university. It says a lot about the monastic existence I led that the wines matured extremely well because what wines like is to slumber somewhere cool, dark, quiet and away from any vibrations. Even in our centrally-heated, cramped and crowded modern living spaces, we can usually find somewhere that vaguely fits that bill.

Good and bad places Don't store your wines in the kitchen. Of all the rooms at home this is the most likely one to have a see-sawing temperature. There are two classic places (excluding under the bed). If you've got a space under the stairs, it's often ideal. And if you've got any kind of old cellar, that's great so long as the central heating boiler isn't down there. Garages can be good, but not if they become boiling hot during the summer. Wardrobes and cubby holes along an exterior wall that never gets the sun are also OK. The loft probably isn't.

Boxes and racking Store all your wines on their sides. Some people say you should store wines like port, Champagne or Hungarian Tokaji standing up. Don't complicate matters. Lay them on their sides. You can just pile them up, but the pile is quite likely to collapse at inconvenient moments. Cardboard wine boxes laid on their side are good, and you *can* pile these on top of each other so long as they are sturdy. But empty the top box first, or everything will collapse.

You can buy wine racks that hold as little as a dozen or as many as several hundred bottles; some are free-standing; others can be nailed to the wall. And if you simply don't have anywhere suitable, but are determined to store and age wines, there are refrigerated wine units can you buy. They're not cheap, but they do work.

If you don't finish the bottle just re-cork it and store it in the fridge. Modern whites, especially from screwcap bottles, can often taste better after a night in the chiller and should easily last a week or two. Rosés are much the same. Champagne will *always* last till the next day kept cold, it'll just be a little less fizzy. And even reds last a day or two kept cold – just remember to take the half-full bottle out of the fridge an hour or two before you want to drink it.

PAYING AN EXPERT

Paying someone else to store your wine is not a problem most of us have. The average time between a bottle being bought and its being drunk is anywhere between 24 seconds and 24 hours, depending upon the thirst of who you talk to. Very few of us are in the game of 'laying down' wine, whether for future enjoyment or sometimes for investment. But if you are, you need to take this storage business seriously. It will keep the wine in better condition, and it'll be worth more.

I didn't. There was a time, long ago, when great wine was cheap (Château Pétrus was only £4 a bottle. I promise. I bought 4 dozen. I wondered what they tasted like. And thereby hangs a tale.) I stored them with amiable florists, charming Cockney cellarmasters with a desperate need to finance a family holiday in the Maldives, best friends of ex-girlfriends and so on. I never paid a penny rent. I never saw my wines again.

So. If you have valuable wines that you intend to age either for your pleasure or to sell – pay an expert to store them for you. Preferably pay an expert who has been in business for quite a long time and has not bunked off with his clients' vinous jewels. *Don't* try to save money on this. The future drinking quality – and the future value – of your wines will depend on who you store them with. The merchant you buy them from should have decent cellaring arrangements. If not, here are a couple of suggestions.

There are commercial bonded warehouses which will store your wine, but the gold standard for storage in the UK is Octavian which is known worldwide and uses cellars and vaults dug deep into Cotswold limestone that were slated for use by the British government in case of nuclear war, so should be able to cope with your wine. You can expect to pay anything from about £9 to £12 a year for each case of wine. Is it worth it? Definitely.

ARE ALL WINES VINTAGE WINES?

In simple terms, a vintage wine is the produce of a single year's harvest. Whatever happens during the growing season will affect the flavour of the grapes, and consequently the wine. The year of the harvest is the vintage date of the wine. In the northern hemisphere, harvest is usually in September and October. In the southern hemisphere it can stretch from as early as January to as late as May.

Where sun is plentiful and rain is limited (so that the vines are nourished by irrigation rather than by the chance occurrence of rain), the difference between each year's harvest is smaller, but even so, no two vintages are quite the same. Nonetheless, if you're buying wine from most parts of Chile, Argentina, California, South Africa or

Australia, the quality differences are usually between good and very good. You could say the same about southern Europe, but the wines will taste different each year. Even here a vintage can be delayed with rain, and certainly a summer can be blasted with drought.

Except for the cheapest examples, most reds, whites and pinks have a vintage date on the bottle, but many sparkling wines don't, and most fortified wines don't. There are usually flavour differences between each harvest. If you are drinking the youngest vintage, this may only be mildly interesting, but for top wines vintage difference can result in big variations of ageability, pleasure and value.

TOO YOUNG, TOO OLD OR JUST READY?
As wine lies in its bottle, it evolves. Tannins soften, acid mellows, red wines grow paler and develop sediment, whites darken to a nutty, rich amber. But older wine is not always better wine and most wines don't need to age. Some wines really can't age. But a surprising number of every sort of wine can age, so here's why.

HOW WINES MATURE
Red wines, when they're very new, are usually dark and purple in colour. Very new white wines usually have almost no colour at all. However, as soon as oxygen in the air comes into contact with the wine, things change, because oxygen immediately interacts with the wine, initially creating extra flavours and perfumes as well as softening the wine's texture, and changing its colour. Red wines gradually lose their intense purpley red and white wines gain a golden or straw hue.

This is all good. But after a while, the oxygen stops improving and the wine starts to turn it bad. Red wines lose their intensity, and the colour goes from purple to blood red, to brick and finally to orange or brown. White wines get darker, going from straw to deeper gold and orange, and finally to brown. Everything will eventually end up brown. The trick with maturing wines is to judge when the oxygen has done maximum good, before it starts to hasten a wine's decline into vinegar – because that's where all wine will finally end up.

> The easiest way to see how oxygen attacks fruit is to cut open an apple or a banana, and leave it for a short while. The apple or banana will rapidly turn brown – that's the oxygen attacking the fruit and breaking it down. The technical term is 'oxidation'.

WINES THAT CAN AGE

Most wines don't need to age and some really can't age. But a surprising number can age. Don't worry if you discover the odd bottle you'd forgotten for a bit. It will probably be OK, but will have lost a little freshness. Wines in screwcaps actually age better than most wines with corks in their bottles.

Don't bother Most cheap wines, wherever they are from, don't need aging. There are some areas of the world that make wines which improve with aging but the cheapest wines even from these regions won't improve.

Red wines need more age than whites In general, red wines need age more than whites, but that doesn't mean that whites can't get better.

France Red Bordeaux wines usually improve with age, as do reds from the Rhône Valley and Burgundy. Some whites from Burgundy, Bordeaux, the Loire Valley and Alsace can get better, as does sweet Sauternes. And Champagne *does* age, whatever the so-called experts say. Good ones age surprisingly well.

Italy Chianti Classico and Brunello often get better after a year or so. Barolo and Amarone definitely improve with time.

Spain Red Rioja and Ribera del Duero like aging, as does Priorat. Sherry is usually released well aged.

Portugal Douro reds often improve with age. Vintage port likes to age and Madeira can last virtually for ever.

New World Wines are usually labelled according to grape variety. Remember, the cheapest ones won't age, but for red wines look out for Cabernet Sauvignon, Shiraz or Syrah (they're the same grape), and Malbec. In general, drink the whites as soon as you've bought them.

YOUNG VERSUS OLD

Ask any wine enthusiast what is the biggest sin in wine drinking and they should answer – drinking a wine when it's too old. If you're one of those lucky people with a cellar, someone who collects and stores wine, the biggest temptation you face is not continually dashing down to pick some lovely mouthful off the shelf without proper preparation. It's not realizing that your lovely, cherished red doesn't go that well with the chicken curry. No. It's keeping the wine too long. All wines have a lifespan, short or long, all wines peak, sooner or later, all wines fade and die. One of the most common excuses for drinking a wine too old is that you were waiting for a special occasion.

Nonsense. Every day can be a special occasion. It's up to you to make it happen. And knowing when a wine is at its peak is often like trying to predict the weather. No one really knows when a wine peaks. No one necessarily knows *what* a wine's peak is – it'll be different for different people. But if you want to make a mistake about when to drink a wine – drink it too young.

A wine which is too young is full of the promise of things to come, will still have lots of life and fruit, and you can make knowing remarks about how well it's developing, if you feel the urge to. A wine which is too old has nothing to offer but regret, a wistful flicker of the flavours and perfumes it once had, a damp-eyed reproach to you for your meanness or carelessness in not opening it much sooner when it still had some of the bloom of youth.

There are a few wines you can take risks with in aging. But most modern wines are good to drink as soon as they hit the shelves. As a general rule, the cheaper the wine, the less chance it has of improving.

Bordeaux Many red Bordeaux wines are built for aging. 5–15 years, can go 20+

Cabernet-based wines These keep their character and often improve. 5–10 years

Rioja Although most Rioja drinks young, good ones age quite well. 5–15 years

Chianti Classico Often softens after a few years. 3–7 years

Port Almost all ports will age in bottle, even tawnies. 5–20 years

White wines Drink young, though an extra year won't harm most of them. The best white Burgundies and Rieslings age well. 3–10 years.

Champagne Almost always able to age 2–3 years, sometimes 5+

VINTAGES DO MATTER FOR SOME WINES

Ask any gardener. Every year is different. One year the tomatoes are better. The next year the cabbages are bigger. The next year there was a massive caterpillar attack. Nature's like that. And grape-growing is nature. However much the big boys try to industrialize the vineyards, try to homogenize the product and try to create wines that never change, nature will try to leave its mark.

Vintages don't matter Those cheap, gaudily-branded wines, usually from the New World, don't change much year by year, simply because the vineyards are managed as industrially as possible, and whatever flavour the wines have is decided by the marketing department rather than the winemaker. There are lots of perfectly legal flavourants, colourants and perfumes available if you want to tinker with the juice. Drink these wines as young as possible.

Vintages do matter But vintages *do* matter for most wines, sometimes only a bit, sometimes a good deal. They used to say that vintages were all the same in the New World. That's tosh. With the ravages of global warming equally evident in both southern and northern hemispheres, and with the dramatic effects of the El Niño and La Niña weather events creating extreme conditions several times a decade, growing conditions in a vineyard can vary wildly year by year.

Vintages matter most where the grapes are at that limit of being able to ripen. This includes northern Portugal (Douro), northern Spain (Rioja), central Italy (Chianti) and northern Italy (Piedmont), western France (Bordeaux and Loire) and northern France (Burgundy and Champagne). All varieties require different amounts of sun and warmth to ripen. Grenache, which needs Mediterranean sun to ripen, couldn't grow successfully in cooler northern France whereas Germany's Riesling, used to chilly conditions, would overripen if you planted it on the Mediterranean coast.

Vintages also matter where wines are being made with the objective of aging them, since some years produce much better flavours in the grapes than others do. In areas, like France's Bordeaux and Burgundy, enthusiasts endlessly discuss the relative merits of different producers in different vintages, and gleefully chart a vintage's progress, up to a plateau of enjoyability, and on to its inevitable decline. Anywhere in northern Europe is likely to show big vintage variation – you only have to live through an English summer to understand that.

> *Where vintages matter most*
> **France** Bordeaux, Burgundy, Champagne, Loire Valley, Northern Rhône
> **England**
> **Germany** Mosel, Rhine
> **Italy** Barolo, Brunello, Chianti, Valpolicella Amarone
> **New Zealand** South Island
> **Portugal** Douro
> **Spain** Rías Baixas, Ribera del Duero, Rioja, Toro
> **USA** New York State, Oregon

FAMOUS OLDER VINTAGES

In Europe's great wine regions, every year's harvest gives a different quality of grapes and so the wines of different years can range from wonderful to pretty poor. If you want to show off a bit, it's not a bad idea to know which years (or vintages) were best for the top wines in some of the classic wine regions. To be honest, most vintages give good wine nowadays and some less famous years turn out far better than expected.

Here is a list of some of the most successful mature vintages to aid your wine cred, as well as good recent vintages, just so you know.

Red Bordeaux 2015, '10, '09, '05, '00, '96, '90, '89, '85, '82

Red Burgundy 2015, '12, '09, '05, '02, '99, '96, '93, '90, '89, '85

Côte-Rôtie (red Rhône) 2015, '13, '12, '11, '10, '09, '07, '05, '02, '99, '98, '95, '91, '88

Champagne 2012, '09, '08, '06, '02, '98, '96, '95, '90, '89

Barolo (Italian red) 2011, '13, '10, '09, '08, '07, '06, '04, '01, '99, '96, '89, '85

Rioja (Spanish red) 2012, '10, '09, '07, '05, '04, '01, '98, '96, '95, '94

Vintage port 2011, '09, '07, '04, '00, '97, '94, '92, '91, '83, '80, '77

BECOMING A GEEK

TASTING WINE

As you try more and more wines,
your awareness of flavour and your
personal preferences will develop.
And the good thing is that you will be
able to apply this knowledge when
choosing wine in a shop, restaurant
or bar.

TASTING VERSUS DRINKING

Tasting versus drinking? Yes, there's a difference. Which one is better? Well, they're both pretty good fun. And if you're careful, you can mix them up a bit. After all, whatever we so-called expert wine tasters say, wine does taste better when you swallow it, not spit it out. We only spit because professional wine-tasting is a pretty full on occupation – I'm sometimes faced with hundreds of wines a day – and you can get seriously clattered if you don't spit out.

So is the difference between tasting and drinking just the 'spitting out' palaver? No. Above all, it's your thought processes, and your objectives when you pour yourself some wine. If you've had a hard day and you simply want a glass or two of grog to relax, 'drinking' it, rather than 'tasting' it, means you don't have to spend time thinking about the wine if you don't want to.

But check out that phrase 'thinking about what you're drinking'. What does that mean? To me, it's the heart of the matter. If you think while you drink you'll be having opinions and coming to conclusions about the flavour of the wine you're drinking, the style, whether you like it or not and why, whether it is value for money, would you buy it again – and we're bang in the middle of 'tasting' a wine rather than just drinking it. You don't have to spit. You just have to think.

So. Pour yourself a glass. Look at the colour – especially with pink and white wines, or with fizz, you can get pleasure and anticipation just by looking at the stuff.

Then smell it. Don't worry too much about smelling fizz unless you like bubbles up your nose – but all other wines have got a smell, for better or worse, and this is part of the pleasure – it's helping you make decisions, and it's adding to the fun a glass of wine can give you. So lower your nose into the top of your glass, and take a good healthy sniff. And then take a second or two to register what the smell is like.

Finally, take a decent – not massive – mouthful. If you gulp it straight back, well, you'll get a fair idea of what it's like. But you'll be missing a lot too. So take some wine in your mouth and hold it there for a few seconds, swirling it around if you like, letting it warm up, letting the flavour become more obvious.

And then you swallow it (or spit it out). But we're not finished. All good wines leave an aftertaste. Take a few seconds to enjoy that as it spreads out from the top of your throat. And hey, you're not just a wine drinker any more, you're a wine taster, too.

YOUR FIRST WINE TASTING

Your first wine tasting is the first time you get a few friends together and say, let's all meet at my place, bring a bottle and we'll all sit round and have a good laugh and learn a bit about what we do like and what we don't. This is how I began learning to taste wine as a student – it didn't do me any harm in the social stakes either. We all had a good time, and we did learn.

If this doesn't sound serious enough for you, there are courses you can sign up for – the Wine & Spirit Education Trust run them worldwide – and there are numerous wine schools keen to enrol you, but I'd leave that till a little later, when you have decided you really *do* want to take this wine knowledge thing further. And I would start around the kitchen table.

Yes, I mean kitchen table. Not a smart dining table in a smart dining room. If your first wine tasting is going to be a success, informality is the key. Most people feel a bit nervous about having to 'taste' wine rather than drink it, having to talk about wine, having to voice an opinion. So get together in the kitchen. If you want to put a bit of spice into things, tell everyone to bring a bottle wrapped in a bag so that you can't see the label. And tell everyone they have to make a comment on each wine – it doesn't matter what they say, but they must say something. It's not always easy finding words to describe wine, so whatever comes into your head first – say it.

Oh. And don't spit. Not to start with. Alcohol is a great loosener of inhibitions and tongues. Someone who is stone cold sober may be too uptight to contribute, but after a glass or so of wine, in vino veritas kicks in and everyone starts speaking their mind. And *then* you can direct people to the sink or to a bucket and suggest that they start spitting. Indeed, it'll all seem part of the fun.

You don't have to cover the labels up, but you'll get more honest opinions if you do, and you'll all learn. But always reveal the label after you've given an opinion on it. Seeing the label helps you remember what you thought about the wine.

Making tasting wine a habit and giving wine a bit of thought while you are drinking it is by far the best method for finding your way around the grapes, regions and styles of the wine world. There are six simple steps: **1** Look at the wine. **2** Give the wine a vigorous swirl to release the locked-in aromas. **3** Stick your nose right into the glass and take a good healthy sniff. **4** Take a decent-sized sip. **5** Draw a little air through your lips and suck it through the wine. **6** If you want to taste more than a few wines in one session, do it the proper way and spit it out so you can keep a clear head.

Talking of which, someone should take some notes. Ideally you all should. Again, it's amazing how much you can forget when you're having a good time. In the cold light of next day, a few scribbled notes may bring it all back to you. So long as they're tasting notes, that is, not just someone's name and a phone number.

TASTE LIKE A PRO

I admit it. We wine tasters can look a bit odd when we're hard at it. All that sniffing and slurping and gurgling – and then there's the spitting. None of this is likely to get you a repeat invitation for supper. But there is method in our madness, so let's give it the once over.

It's pretty easy to decide whether we like a wine or not – we can all do it, and it probably takes us about 10 seconds flat. But when I'm wine tasting I've often got lots of other things to consider. Is it typical of its grape variety and area? Does it have any faults? Is it good value for money? Will it age well? What sort of food might suit it best? All that sort of thing. And this takes concentration. Which explains the spitting out. The more alcohol you swallow, the less you're able to concentrate – and serious wine tasting is hard work. Stop laughing at the back of the class.

1. Look at the wine With the exception of a few of the so-called 'natural' wines (see page 56), wine should be clear, not cloudy. If you have an old red wine, this may have thrown sediment. That's normally a good sign, but you should stand these old bottles upright for a few hours and then pour carefully. You'll get almost all the wine out starbright.

Looking at the wine can tell you about the age – whites are greener and paler when young, and go deeper and more golden with age. Red wines are darker, more purple when they're young and get lighter with age, as well as losing the purple as the red turns to blood red, brick red and eventually fades away. The best way to judge a wine's – particularly a red's – colour is to place a sheet of white paper on the table, then tilt the glass of wine so that the liquid spreads up towards the rim, and gaze at it thoughtfully with the paper as a background. All the nuances of colour will become clear.

2. Give the wine a vigorous swirl Nearly all wines give off a smell; some give off a positive pong. This can be really attractive, so smelling it is a pleasure. If you're a pro, the smell can also alert you to any winemaking techniques – like the use of oak barrels which give off a spicy, vanilla-ish smell, and also to wine faults like sourness, oxidation and mustiness. Some wine tasters have a special note they use after smelling some wines. DNPIM. Do Not Put In Mouth. One taster goes even further. AE. Auto Eject. Wine tasting's not all fun.

Back to smelling. Pour yourself a decent measure – a mouthful or two. Then gently swirl the glass. This'll take a bit of practise; I'd suggest you practise with water rather than red wine until you've mastered the extremely light touch needed to swirl some wine round the glass. It's like fly-fishing – the less effort you make, the better the end result. The reason you're doing this is because wine aromas are volatile, so if you swirl the wine around, the aromas will get pushed up to the top of the glass.

3. Stick your nose right into the glass And that's when you dip your nose into the glass and take a good healthy sniff. Our sense of smell is our most ancient sense, but it's also underused by us. Even so, it's linked to memory and emotion, so take a sniff and try to catch your first impression. It could be of a fruit or a scent, or a childhood memory or an adolescent disaster. Emotions have smells, experiences are brought back by smell. If you try to catch that fleeting first impression, and are absolutely true to yourself when describing it, you'll be on the way to becoming a smart wine taster.

4. Take a decent-sized sip Now you put it in your mouth. Take a reasonable amount in. The warmth inside your mouth will wake up the flavours in the wine. But it's your nasal cavity, not your mouth, that's doing the tasting. Our tongue can really only taste five things: bitterness, sweetness, acidity and salt, and the ill-defined savoury flavour called umami (things like cheese and soy sauce have quite a lot of this). But inside our nasal cavity there are 5 million – yes, 5 million – receptor sites, each one looking for individual smells. Scientists reckon we can detect over 10,000 odours. They've already identified hundreds of the flavours and smells in wine. So. Back to our mouth.

All the while that the wine is in your mouth, you're still breathing, aren't you? Each inward breath draws those warm aromas up from your mouth into your nasal cavity.

5. Draw a little air through your lips and suck it through the wine
You can maximize this transfer of aromas by breathing in through

your mouth. And that is a bit tricky. You sometimes see wine tasters pursing their lips and rather rowdily inhaling. They'll be breathing in through a mouthful of wine. It really wakes the wine up, but you need to practise. As with most tasting techniques, start with mouthfuls of water. And a) don't choke, b) don't lean your head forward because the liquid will spill all down your chin.

You're almost there. While the wine is in your mouth, try to gauge the effect of acidity and bitter tannins on your tongue and palate. All wines need acidity, and red wines must have some bitterness from the grape skins. It's all a matter of balance. If you practise, you'll start to make up your own mind about what seems balanced to you. And if you're tasting very young wines with the objective of judging how well they'll age, acidity and tannin are important, and will be more marked at an early stage. Tannin in particular drops away in a good wine with a bit of age.

6. *Swallow or spit* And one more thing. Either swallow – and then take a few seconds to react to the aftertaste – or spit. Honestly, I know it looks terrible, but you have to do this if you're trying any great number of wines. I'd say any number greater than a dozen, and you need to spit so that you can keep a clear head and don't end up face down in the spittoon. Look, we've all spat things out. It's just the same with wine, so let's not try to complicate matters. But, once again, practise with water. One wine-writing friend of mine used to lie in the bath practising her spitting. I presume the bath was full of water, not wine, but you never know.

WHY BOTHER WITH TASTING NOTES?

If you think you can remember all the nuances displayed by a clutch of different wines which you somehow managed to swallow rather than spit out, and whose bottles you drained although you swore you wouldn't, if you think that in the cold light of tomorrow you'll remember which was which and what was what, fine, don't make any tasting notes. But from my fairly comprehensive experience, I can promise you that even when the evening went on way too long and you went far too far, some decent tasting notes can bring the flavours and personalities of wines back into focus even on the murkiest of mornings after.

I mean, we all know that alcohol doesn't help our ability to remember – although it does help our ability to make things up. Put these two together and a glass or two of wine will help you have a much more imaginative reaction to wines, which you will then forget – unless you write stuff down.

It doesn't have to be complicated. You can simply have three headings: colour, smell and taste. Or you can forget about colour. And you can combine smell and taste. You can just write a few simple words: the name of the wine, a couple of comments like 'Oh, zingy, fruity, chewy, awesome, yuck...' If you find more specific flavours, do write them down: blackcurrant, chocolate, raspberry, smoky, apple peel... Be brave. Any flavour you think you find is there – for you, at least. These really will help you remember the wine next time you look at the notes.

WORDS TO DESCRIBE WINE

There's more to describing wine than saying it's good or bad. Tasting terms are a way of sharing our perceptions of a wine's qualities; they should never be a secret code for experts. Fruit flavours are direct comparisons, so if I know the fruit, I will recognize the flavour you are talking about. The same goes for honey or nuts. These less obvious terms are useful too.

Aggressive A wine with acid that makes your gums sting or that dries up the back of your throat due to an excess of tannin.

Appley Loads of dry white wines taste of apples – whether sweet or sour, their flesh, core or peel, cooked or raw. Try to be specific.

Aromatic All wines have an aroma, but an aromatic wine is particularly pungent, floral or spicy, and is usually from an aromatic grape variety like Gewürztraminer.

Astringent A wine in which the mouthdrying effect of tannin is very marked.

Big A full-bodied wine with lots of everything: fruit flavour, acidity, tannin and alcohol.

Blackcurrant That's cooked blackcurrant as in jam.

Bold A wine with distinct, easily understood flavours.

Brioche Slightly sweet but soft, yeast cake crust.

Buttery Oak barrels and malolactic fermentation can both give a buttery taste.

Chewy Wine with a lot of tannin and strong flavour, but which is not aggressive.

Chocolatey Rich, warm-country reds often taste chocolatey; heavily toasted oak barrels can add a chocolate taste and texture.

Clean Wine free of bacterial and chemical faults. Also describes simple, refreshing wines.

Complex A wine that has layer upon layer of flavours.

Crisp A refreshing white wine with good acidity.

Deep Subtle, rich; allied to complex.

Dry Not at all sweet.

Dull A wine with no well-defined, pleasing flavours. Often a sign of too much exposure to oxygen.

Dusty A dry, slightly earthy taste sometimes found in reds. Can be very attractive if combined with good fruit.

Earthy A smell and taste of damp earth – appealing in some French reds from the Loire Valley and Bordeaux.

Farmyardy Self-explanatory. Rather a lot of cows and pigs around.

Fat Full-bodied, unctuous.

Firm Well-balanced, well-defined wine; the opposite of flabby.

Flabby Lacking in acidity, feeble.

Floral Several whites have an aroma like flowers or blossom.

Focused A wine in which all the flavours are well defined.

Fresh Young wine, with lively fruit flavours and good acidity.

Full A weighty feel in the mouth.

Grassy Commonly used though not strictly accurate term for the green leaf, lime zest or capsicum (green pepper) flavours typical of Sauvignon Blanc.

Green Can mean unripe, in which case it's pejorative. But green leaf flavours are common in cool-climate reds, and greenness in association with flavours such as gooseberries or apples implies the fresh, tangy flavours found in many white wines.

Hard A red with a lot of tannin or a white with too much acid. Uncompromising rather than aggressive, but rarely enjoyable.

Jammy Red wine in which the fruit has the boiled, cooked flavours of jam. This can be nice or it can be cloying.

Light Low alcohol or little body. Not necessarily a bad thing.

Meaty A heavy red wine with solid, chunky flavours. A few wines actually do taste of grilled meat or bloody beef.

Minerally How you might imagine a lick of flint or chalk to taste. Common in wines from Chablis and the Loire Valley in France, Germany and Austria.

Neutral Little distinctive flavour.

Oaky The slightly sweet vanilla flavour in reds and whites that have been fermented and/or aged in new oak barrels. Oak also adds tannin.

Petrolly A surprisingly attractive petrol- or kerosene-like smell that develops in mature wines made from Riesling.

Piercing Usually refers to high acidity. But vibrant fruit flavours can also be piercing.

Plum A general term for indistinct, quite ripe, round, dark red flavours. E.g. Malbec may taste of damsons.

Powerful A wine with plenty of everything, particularly alcohol.

Prickly Slight fizziness caused by residual carbon dioxide gas, often meaning that fermentation is not quite finished. Very refreshing in simple whites but usually considered a fault in red wines.

Raspberry A delightfully assertive flavour in some red wines. Cabernet Franc tastes of raspberry, as do some northern Italian and Austrian reds, and some Beaujolais and Burgundy.

Rich Full, well-flavoured, with plenty of alcohol.

Ripe Wine made from well-ripened grapes has good fruit flavour. Unripe wines can taste green and stalky.

Rounded Any wine in which the flavour seems satisfyingly complete, with no unpleasant sharpness.

Soft A wine without harsh tannins or too much acidity, making it an easy-going drink. Often a good thing, but a wine can be too soft.

Spicy Exotic fragrances and flavours common in Gewürztraminer; also the tastes of pepper, cinnamon or clove in reds such as Australian Shiraz. Spiciness can be an effect of oak aging.

Steely Good acidity and a wine that is firm and lean, may be minerally but not thin.

Stony A dry, chalky-white taste, like minerally but without quite the excitement.

Strawberryish Lots of soft reds taste of strawberry, especially Garnacha, Pinot Noir and some red Burgundy.

Structured 'Plenty of structure' refers to a wine with a well-developed backbone of acidity and tannin, but enough fruit to stand up to it.

Supple Of texture not flavour, both vigorous and smooth.

Sweet Not only a wine with high levels of sugar, but also the rich and ripe quality of some of the fruit flavours in many modern dry wines.

Tart A very sharp, acid taste like an unripe apple.

Thin, lean, stringy Terms for high-acid wine lacking in flavour.

Toasty A flavour like buttered toast that results from maturing a wine in oak barrels.

Upfront A wine that wears its heart on its sleeve: expect obvious flavours, not subtle ones, but sometimes that's just what you want.

WINE FAULTS

We're talking about the big faults here, not minor hiccups. There aren't many to worry about, so let's get stuck in.

Use your eyes

Wines should be clear and bright in the glass. If an old red wine is slightly cloudy, that's probably the wine's sediment getting stirred up. You need to pour old wines pretty carefully to avoid this, but a touch of sediment won't hurt the flavour. The only time a young wine should be cloudy is if you've ordered a 'natural' or an 'orange' wine (see pages 56–57). They're a bit of a minority taste – often being a bit cloudy and a bit cidery (the white wines can even be chewy). And, unless you're ready for the experience, you won't miss much by steering clear of them.

Generally if a dry white is getting a deep golden/orange hue, it's too old (white wines deepen in colour as they age). If a red wine has developed an orange or brownish hue it will probably be too old (red wines get paler with age). Brown tinges usually mean wine has oxidized from too much air contact or too much heat when it was being stored. That said, the best sherry and Madeira can have a brown colour, and tawny port can have a chestnut hue.

Use your nose and taste buds

'Corked' The big wine fault that can strike even the finest of wines is the curse of 'corked'. A 'corked' wine is one where the cork in the bottle was infected by fungus and the wine will taste musty, damp, stale. I used to have an old football shirt I never got round to washing. Yuck. Corked wine was exactly like that. No one knows quite how much 'corked' wine exists, but the figure could be between 1% and 3%. It used to be far more than this, and even the most expensive bottles can be afflicted. Screwcaps are completely inert and are the best closure for most wines.

Oxidation Wine shouldn't smell like sherry unless it *is* sherry. Oxidized wine smells like brown sherry or Madeira, or it can smell of burnt jam or old brown fruit like dried figs, prunes or raisin.

Vinegar Vinegar is wine that has gone sour. Wine should not smell like that.

Sulphur If the wine smells of rotten eggs, it has developed hydrogen sulphide during winemaking – and that's a fault. If it smells of struck matches, that's a different sort of sulphur. Sulphur (nowadays in the form of sulphur dioxide) has been used as a wine antiseptic and antioxidant since Roman times. If the winery has used a bit too much, the first glass of wine from a bottle may have this sulphurous smell, but it often blows away in a few minutes – especially if you swirl the wine about. Some white Burgundies and Chardonnays are made on purpose to have a slight whiff of struck match about them.

WHAT IS A BLIND TASTING?

There are two sorts of blind tasting. One is a competitive blind tasting. This is where you try to guess the identity of a glass of wine. It's a sort of sport, just no physical exertion, but the objective is definitely to win, to make the largest number of most accurate guesses as to what different wines' identities are. You're not shown the label – obviously – you're not shown the bottle shape – you just have an array of glasses of wine, and you're trying to get more marks than anyone else in the room. Can be fun. Can be a nightmare.

The other sort of blind tasting is rather more important. This is where you are trying to judge a wine's quality in as impartial a way as possible. And the most important factor in being impartial about a glass of red or white liquid sitting in front of you is that you *don't* know the identity of the wine. And that's the whole essence of a 'blind tasting'. Most professional tasters use this method when choosing wines to buy.

To be honest, you *could* do the whole thing blindfold, but you'd end up knocking over the glasses and making an awful mess. Much better to have your eyes wide open, but either put all the bottles in plastic or paper bags, or wrap them in anything that will obscure the label. All wine competitions of any value judge all their wines 'blind' like this, with wines being given a code or number. Sometimes you don't even know the style of the wine being judged, but more likely you will know what the category is, probably what the vintage is, sometimes what the price band is, and then you judge and mark the wine with as little prejudice as you can muster.

It works. But it's tough. You really have to concentrate when you can't see the label. It's the best way to judge, and it's the best way to learn. But I believe that if you want to cement that knowledge, once you've judged the wine and marked it, then it really helps to see the label. The visual image helps fix the memory of the flavour and the wine's quality in your mind. I can still remember the label of some of the wines I learned on. The flavour still keeps flooding back. But if you see the label first, even the flintiest of wine tasters will be swayed to some extent.

In the old days they used to say that the best way to become good at blind wine tasting was to bribe the butler. Which rather tells you how far we've come since then. Does anyone know anyone who HAS a butler any more?

IMPRESS YOUR FRIENDS

I've just plucked a few wine terms out of the air which might help you impress your drinking mates. Since a lot of wine tasting terms rely on borrowed language (like saying a wine tastes of various fruits, blackcurrant or strawberry, for instance, when the wine doesn't contain any fruit except grapes), or on our first impressions (which could be anything from a damp springtime meadow to a winter wood fire or the emotional memory of someone important in our lives) – I've left out such words and phrases.

The following are just a few terms used by the professionals which you could sprinkle into a wine conversation and gain a few bragging rights.

Profound This means the wine is serious, demands contemplation, discussion, dissection of its component parts rather than an emotional response. It could also just mean that the wine is a dense, monolithic old thing that no one can make head or tail of.

Needs keeping A useful phrase, particularly for red wines that are tough, tannic, teeth-staining and not much fun to drink. Indeed, such wines might well improve. But it's also a polite way of complimenting a wine that seems to be short on fruit and fun.

Interesting This is a wonderful term. It should mean that the wine possesses loads of features that fascinate us and which we can't wait to discuss. It should be a compliment leading to a boisterous exchange of opinions. But in reality it's often a polite way of saying you either don't like the wine, or you certainly don't get why other people do.

Linear Now we're getting serious. This can apply to reds or whites, and suggests that the wine is gaunt, austere, haughty (those are actually three rather good words that cover a multitude of sins). An acid wine, a thin wine, a wine short on fruit and perfume but long on acidity and tannin and mineral tastes. A wine without any flesh, without any curves.

Mineral Mineral is an excellent term because a lot of wines do have a taste a bit like earth or damp chalk or wet stones. Well, what we *imagine* to be those flavours, because scientists tell us wine can't pick up flavours from the different components in soil, and the term mineral is being pooh-poohed at the moment. I'd stick with it when you're faced with quite a few dry reds and whites, particularly from France and Italy. And if your friends say, oh, the grape can't pick up mineral traces, freeze them a withering smile and say wine description is all about suggestion, not reality.

Reductive This is an interesting term, and quite useful for impressing. It means that a wine has a slightly savoury, sometimes meaty, sulphurous smell, often caused by traces of hydrogen sulphide and a slight lack of oxygen during winemaking and wine maturing. Screwcap wines are a bit prone to it, and some top Chardonnays and white Burgundies on purpose create a flavour a bit like struck matches that can be called reductive.

TCA This is a big one. TCA stands for – wait for it – Trichloroanisole 2-4-6. It's the chemical that gives a nasty damp musty flavour to wines that are described as 'corked'. TCA is the chemical in the cork that mucks up the wine. Your friends can say 'corked'. You can say, 'touch of TCA'.

Methoxypyrazine Here's another scientific beauty. Methoxypyrazines are green, slightly underripe elements in red and white wines. In areas of the world where grapes can't ripen properly, or in really terrible vintages, these green, stalky, leafy, sappy flavours dominate the wine and spoil it. But in cool places like New Zealand, Canada, New York and the chilliest bits of Chile, Australia, South Africa, France and Italy – a seasoning of these green, leafy, lime zesty, apple peely flavours is what makes them 'cool-climate' and refreshing. Some wine buffs say they're a fault. Fight your corner.

Thiol OK. Another bit of science. Thiols are also found in cool-climate areas, and some winemakers are convinced that they are the secret of making, say, really exciting Sauvignon Blanc. They can be – when they taste of things like passion fruit. But they are just as likely to make a wine taste of a football player's sweat. So if you see a wine with that 'unwashed' character – 'hmm, a touch of thiols here' will impress the table.

pH And more science. pH is one of those things that really is quite difficult to explain. It's sort of a measure of alkalinity versus acidity, with neutral being at 7. To generalize, the lower your pH, the more the acidity will dominate your wine. The higher the pH, the flatter it will seem. Almost all wine is measured between 3 and 4. pH will be lower for whites than reds, and in general wines with low pH will be brighter, snappier, sharper, and wines with high pH will be lusher, richer and broader. And on the whole 'low pH' is more of a compliment than 'high pH'.

Malolactic Ah, another juicy scientific term. The 'malolactic' fermentation used to be called the 'second fermentation'. The 'first fermentation' turns sugar into alcohol. This 'second fermentation' isn't really a fermentation, it's the result of bacterial action converting malic acid (which tastes like green apples) into lactic acid (which tastes like milk or cream). In other words, it's nothing to do with creating more alcohol, but has a big role to play in turning acid wine into something softer. Most wines start out with significant levels of sharp malic acid. Red wines almost always need to soften up by undergoing this 'malolactic' fermentation, which is quite natural, but you can induce it.

White wines are different. Sometimes you want to keep that appley acid – like in Sauvignon Blancs or Rieslings – but sometimes you want to convert it to softer lactic acid in wines like Chardonnay or white Burgundy. In the winery, you can stop the malolactic or encourage it, entirely depending on what style of wine you want. If you think your white is too soft and creamy, you can say, 'hmm – too much malolactic'. If it's raw, you can say the reverse.

START YOUR OWN COLLECTION

This is what some wine lovers dream about – they have visions of gallery upon gallery of cobwebby, candlelit cellars, packed full of the vinous gems of generations, every one maturing to perfection, ripe to be plucked from its slumbers and taken to the table, where it will perform beyond all expectation.

It's a lovely dream. And best to leave it like that – as a dream. Because most of us have absolutely no need of a wine collection. The supermarkets have a wide range of good wine. Independent merchants have a wide range of good to excellent wine. If they're not enough, there are wine clubs and wine societies that will draw us into their bosom, make us feel we belong in the fraternity of wine, and sell us a wide range of just about everything we could wish for.

Yes, yes, but what if you really, truly *want* to have your own wine collection? OK. Just so long as you're doing this for the fun of it – and I do sympathize – every cool nook and cranny in my house has got wine bottles of every sort hiding there. Don't expect the wines to become far more valuable and provide a pension nest egg. They won't.

The pros and cons Will starting a wine collection give you enormous joy over the years as the wines mature to far finer flavours than they had when they were in the shops? Yes it will. Will some wines fail to get better so that you wish you'd never bought them? Yes again. Will it save you money over the years? Well, if you've got cool, dark spaces at home for storing the wines, and if you presume – correctly, I'm afraid – that most good wines get more expensive over the years, yes, it will save you money.

Do it for the love of wine I really wouldn't do it to save money. I do it for the sheer love of the wine, for the joy of having a wide selection of wines – mostly under the stairs, in my case. I don't have a splendiferous array of smart wooden cases of 12 bottles – most of my treasures are in two or three bottle lots. They're not all Bordeaux and Burgundy – my friends are always amazed or alarmed by the breadth of the selection they get when they come round to my place – anything from Denmark and Switzerland to Canada and Uruguay and Namibia (yes, really). I have got Bordeaux and Burgundy, I've got Rioja, Chianti and vintage port. But it's the whole wide world of wine that I collect. And if *my* delight is anything to go by, you should give it a go.

WINE AND FASHION

Does fashion in wine matter? Do you have to be a slavish follower of wine fashion? Well, what's your view on clothes fashion or music fashion? What's your view on visiting the coolest pub or club or restaurant? Do you relentlessly follow the latest fad in food, or do you go on eating what you like?

'What you like.' That's the crucial thing. Sometimes the things we like are in fashion, sometimes they're not. And wine is just the same. Luckily, fads normally affect the lower end of the market. At one time Muscadet was a really cool dry white, Beaujolais was a hipster red, Portuguese pink (Mateus, anybody?) was cool, and any German wines were super-fashionable. And they all fell from favour so that the coolsters wouldn't be seen dead drinking them.

Well, Portuguese pink is still just a perfectly nice pink wine and you might say – why did it ever get fashionable? OK. Why did white Zinfandel get fashionable? Why are Pinot Grigio and Prosecco fashionable? These things happen. But Muscadet can be one of France's most easy-going, food-friendly, low alcohol and *unoaked* white wines. That should be right in-fashion now. If it isn't, you should take pride in drinking Muscadet for what it is, not for its image.

Beaujolais is the same. Juicy, crunchy, low in alcohol, wonderfully refreshing, unoaked again – what's not to like? Well, somehow people still remember the über-fad of Beaujolais Nouveau – which made Beaujolais just about the most famous red wine in the world for a generation – then killed it stone dead. Beaujolais became famous for a reason. It was one of France's most delicious red wines. It'll come back into fashion. Get there first.

And as for Germany. A century ago German wines were more revered than any others. Two World Wars didn't help, but the wines were still admired and respected – until the 1970s and 1980s when Niersteiner, Liebfraumilch and Piesporter Michelsberg swamped the world market with semi-sweet, sulphurous muck – and Germany's reputation was ruined. Yet Germany is one of Europe's great wine producers. Austria had its reputation destroyed by an anti-freeze scandal in the 1980s. Yet it is now one of Europe's great wine producers. I could go on.

Only follow fashion if it leads you to new and exciting places. The whole New World revolution relied on fashion for its success – New Zealand Sauvignon Blanc, Australian Chardonnay and Shiraz and Chilean Merlot. So drink what pleases you. And wines that are out of fashion are often cheaper and the producers are often making far more effort to excite you than the fashionista wine producers are.

FINDING OUT MORE

Wines are reviewed in many different places – TV, radio, in newspapers and magazines, and on dedicated websites and blogs, but sharing your information with friends is one of the best ways of gathering recommendations.

WORLD WIDE WEB OF WINE

I doubt if anyone doesn't now use the internet for some of their wine activities, whether it's sourcing wine to buy, comparing the prices of wine or using a mixture of Google and specific blogs and websites to find out about wine. As with just about every other commodity, we can research any object, buy whatever we want and at the fairest price without ever leaving our desk at home, or without taking our eyes off our smartphone screen when we're on the move. If we're into peer to peer chat, and would prefer to get our recommendations from our supposed peers – even if we've never met any of them – the web is awash with opportunities.

But if I can just put a slight dampener on all this digital joy, one of the great things about wine is that it should be about human interaction. That's *actual* human interaction: tasting, discussing, comparing, looking at the labels, holding the bottles, anticipating the pop of the cork, the glug glug of the wine being poured, the first smell wafting out of the glass, the smile on everyone's faces as they take the first mouthful…

Now I'm not saying the internet doesn't offer a version of all these things. But I think I'd still prefer to find a wine merchant I can relate to – who will almost certainly sell online anyway, but hopefully will also be a friendly 'real' person, likely to open bottles for tasting and chat about stuff face to face. Use the internet as a tool, but don't forget that wine is a very human pleasure all to do with sharing, friendship, laughter and indulgence. Those are all things best enjoyed in person and in company.

LOCAL WINE SOCIETIES

If you're keen on something – be it gardening, football, stamp collecting, choral singing or mudwrestling (well, perhaps not mudwrestling) – one of your first decisions would be to see if there is a local club, society, group or choir to join. Wine's no different. Wine societies are not quite so common as gardening clubs, but most reasonable-sized towns will have some sort of wine society. The society's objective will be to act as a social centre for people who are interested in wine, to provide regular events, usually centred on tastings and meals, sometimes to organize trips, and often to help with education. The thing about wine is, you gotta practise. You can read all you like, but to learn anything worthwhile, you must open bottles, ideally with like-minded friends, drink the wines, and talk about them, enjoy them and, hopefully, remember them. Then, if you read about the wines, it'll all make far more sense.

There are one or two big international wine societies – the International Wine & Food Society is one – and there are successful operations run by national newspapers: *The Sunday Times* Wine Club is a good example. The Wine Society is an excellent British operation.

And many big companies or government departments may have wine societies. The British Civil Service used to have a very active wine society, as did ICI, Britain's biggest chemicals company (they probably still do).

So, check out your workplace or go on the internet to see if your local town has a society. And join. If you like the people, if they organize interesting tastings, if they make your life more fun, stick with it. If not, well, you haven't lost anything, and you'll have drunk a few wines you might never otherwise have tried.

WINE FESTIVALS

There seem to be more and more of these every year. That's great news because wine festivals are seriously good fun. You'll pay a reasonable entrance fee – but don't expect it to be too cheap. The better festivals charge more but then it's all free once you are inside – anywhere from dozens to several hundred wines to taste, producers to meet, competitions to enter and experiments to try. Most festivals have sessions between three and four hours long. That's usually enough if you're not spitting. Well, swallow some of it – fine – but there will be spittoons all over the place, and I strongly recommend you use them as often as possible. Wine festivals are a great chance to learn about different wines as well as to have fun with friends. Don't spoil it by having a skinful and waking up the next day with a parched throat and a thick head.

Some generic wine bodies – for example, New Zealand, South Africa, Chile and Portugal – organize wine shows for the public in the evening after their trade events. Several supermarkets also run wine festivals. Groups of wine professionals run festivals, too – I am part of the Three Wine Men, featuring, well, me and two friends.

Wine walks At most festivals you'll have the chance to go on wine walks with experts. You'll need to book as most wine walks will only be for a small number of people. What happens is that you tag along with the expert who takes you to a variety of producers. The expert tells you about the wine, the producer adds depth and inside knowledge and you learn – from the horse's mouth, so to speak. Most wine walks last for 30 minutes or so. They are worth doing.

WINE TOURING

It is completely, utterly, absolutely worth going on a wine tour. You can taste different wines at home till your tongue disintegrates. You can read purple prose about vineyards and winemakers until you're cross-eyed. You can even attend wine tastings and meet producers – that's pretty exciting – but nothing quite beats getting to the vineyards, walking through the cellars, waiting in anticipation as the winemaker dips his pipette into a barrel and draws out a precious sample of his new wine, made from grapes grown just a stone's throw away. Wine will never taste the same again.

When you drive down the lanes of Burgundy or Bordeaux and see the names of famous properties and villages on the road signs, you'll feel closer to these wines and understand them better than you ever could before.

When you venture deep into the chilly caves driven deep into the hillsides of Champagne, when you realise that the Tuscan hills are even more beautiful than they ever were in an advert, when you follow the course of the Douro River in Portugal or the Mosel River in Germany and marvel that any human being could work these glorious but forbiddingly steep slopes – when you indulge in any of these joys, and a whole host of others too – you will kindle an intense love of wine that you simply can't achieve from your own armchair. So, yes, do go on wine tours. They're wonderful.

There are specialist companies with long experience who run fantastic tours year after year. Specialist wine tours are a fantastic way to learn about wine in a way you'll never forget, and it's all done for you – visits planned, experts to show you around, translators on hand – but independent travellers can have just as much fun, too. National newspapers may also run tours and the large national wine societies do as well. My first wine trips were to Bordeaux and Burgundy. I've never forgotten them.

WINE CRUISES, CYCLE TOURS AND MORE

An increasing number of river and ocean cruises offer wine options, with tastings on board and visits to wineries and estates on land. They are well worth doing. I've done quite a few and had a marvellous time. Though I have to admit at the end of a 'wine' day on board, I'm usually to be found cradling an ice cold Martini rather than yet another glass of wine.

You can take cruises down rivers like the Mosel or Rhine, the Danube
or the Rhône, or you can sea cruise and drop into any wine region
near the coast, like Bordeaux along the Gironde estuary, and Jerez
which is near Cadiz in south-west Spain.

Many vineyards are in visually thrilling locations, but they are also
often on steep slopes. If you're feeling fit, cycling is a fantastic way
to visit vineyards – you feel as though you have earned your tasting
through the exertions of the ride. And being out in the open air is
much more fun than being cooped up in a car.

Just for the record – Bordeaux's Médoc is very famous and very flat,
Burgundy is gently sloping, Rioja and Chianti are much hillier, while
the Douro and Mosel valleys are so steep that even the mountain
goats get arthritis.

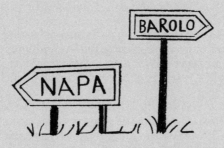

QUICK GUIDE TO
NAMES IN WINE

This is not an exhaustive list of wine
names but includes those often seen
on wine lists or those you might
come across when buying wine.

ARGENTINA
Buenos Aires
Mendoza
• Uco Valley
Patagonia
• Neuquén
La Rioja
Salta
San Juan

AUSTRALIA
New South Wales
• Canberra
  District
• Hunter Valley
• Mudgee
• New England
  Highlands
• Orange
• Hilltops
• Riverina
• Tumburumba
Queensland
South Australia
• Adelaide Hills
• Barossa
• Clare Valley
• Coonawarra
• Eden Valley
• Fleurieu
  Peninsula
• Langhorne
  Creek
• Limestone Coast
• McLaren Vale
• Padthaway
• Riverland

Tasmania
• Coal River
• East Coast
• Huon Valley
Victoria
• Beechworth
• Bendigo
• Geelong
• Gippsland
• Grampians and
  Pyrenees
• Heathcote
• Macedon
  Ranges
• Mornington
  Peninsula
• Rutherglen
• Yarra Valley
Western Australia
• Great Southern
• Manjimup
• Margaret River
• Pemberton
• Swan District

AUSTRIA
Burgenland
Carnuntum
Kamptal
Kremstal
• Neusiedlersee
Niederösterreich
Steiermark
Thermenregion
Wachau
Wien

BRAZIL
Vale do São
Francisco
Planalto Catarinense
Rio Grande do Sul
Serra do Sudeste

CANADA
British Columbia
• Okanagan
  Valley
Ontario
• Niagara
  Peninsula
• Prince Edward
  County

CHILE
Atacama
Aconcagua
• Aconcagua
  Valley
• Casablanca
  Valley
• Leyda Valley
• San Antonio
  Valley
Central Valley
• Cachapoal
  Valley
• Colchagua
  Valley
• Curicó Valley
• Lontué Valley
• Maipo Valley
• Maule Valley
  (Cauquenes)

- Rapel Valley

Coquimbo
- Choapa Valley
- Elquí Valley
- Limarí Valley

South
- Bío Bío
- Itata Valley
- Malleco

CHINA
Hebei
Ningxia
Shandong
Shanxi
Xinjiang
Yunnan

FRANCE
Alsace
Bordeaux
- Barsac
- Blaye-Côtes de Bordeaux
- Cadillac-Côtes de Bordeaux
- Canon-Fronsac
- Castillon-Côtes de Bordeaux
- Cérons
- Côtes de Bourg
- Entre-Deux-Mers
- Francs-Côtes de Bordeaux
- Fronsac
- Graves

- Haut-Médoc
- Lalande-de-Pomerol
- Listrac-Médoc
- Loupiac
- Margaux
- Médoc
- Moulis
- Pauillac
- Pessac-Léognan
- Pomerol
- Premières Côtes de Bordeaux
- St-Émilion
- St-Estèphe
- St-Julien
- Ste-Croix-du-Mont
- Sauternes

Beaujolais
- Brouilly
- Chénas
- Côte de Brouilly
- Fleurie
- Chiroubles
- Juliénas
- Morgon
- Moulin-à-Vent
- Régnié
- St-Amour

Burgundy
- Aloxe-Corton
- Auxey-Duresses
- Bâtard-Montrachet
- Beaune
- Blagny

- Bonnes-Mares
- Bourgogne
- Bourgogne-Côte Chalonnaise
- Bourgogne-Côte d'Or
- Bourgogne Hautes Côtes de Beaune, Hautes-Côtes de Nuits
- Chablis
- Chambertin
- Chambolle-Musigny
- Chassagne-Montrachet
- Chorey-lès-Beaune
- Clos des Lambrays
- Clos de la Roche
- Clos St-Denis
- Clos de Tart
- Clos de Vougeot
- Corton, Corton-Charlemagne
- Côte de Beaune, de Beaune-Villages, de Nuits-Villages
- Coteaux Bourguignons
- Échézeaux
- Fixin
- Gevrey-Chambertin
- Givry

- Irancy
- Ladoix
- Mâcon, Mâcon-Villages
- Maranges
- Marsannay
- Mercurey
- Meursault
- Montagny
- Monthelie
- Montrachet
- Morey-St-Denis
- Musigny
- Nuits-St-Georges
- Pernand-Vergelesses
- Pommard
- Pouilly-Fuissé, Pouilly-Vinzelles
- Puligny-Montrachet
- Richebourg
- la Romanée, la Romanée-Conti, Romanée-St-Vivant
- Rully
- St-Aubin
- St-Bris
- St-Romain
- St-Véran
- Santenay
- Savigny-lès-Beaune
- la Tâche
- Viré-Clessé
- Volnay
- Vosne-Romanée
- Vougeot

Champagne
- Côte des Blancs
- Montagne de Reims
- Vallée de la Marne

Jura
- Arbois
- Chateau-Chalon
- Côtes du Jura
- l'Etoile

Languedoc-Roussillon
- Banyuls
- Blanquette de Limoux
- Cabardès
- la Clape
- Collioure
- Coteaux du Languedoc
- Corbières
- Côtes Catalanes
- Fitou
- Grès de Montpellier
- Limoux
- Maury
- Minervois
- Muscat de Frontignan, de Rivesaltes, de St-Jean-de-Minervois

- Pézenas
- Pic St-Loup
- Picpoul de Pinet
- Rivesaltes
- Roussillon, Côtes du Roussillon
- St-Chinian
- Terrasses du Larzac

Loire Valley
- Bonnezeaux
- Bourgueil
- Cheverny
- Chinon
- Côte Roannaise
- Coteaux de l'Aubance
- Coteaux du Layon
- Jasnières
- Menetou-Salon
- Montlouis-sur-Loire
- Muscadet
- Pouilly-Fumé, Pouilly-sur-Loire
- Quarts de Chaume
- Quincy
- Reuilly
- St-Nicolas-de-Bourgueil
- Sancerre
- Saumur, Saumur-

Champigny,
Saumur
Mousseux
- Touraine
- Vouvray
Provence
- Bandol
- Bellet
- Les Baux-de-
Provence
- Bouches-du-
Rhône
- Cassis
- Coteaux d'Aix-
en-Provence
- Coteaux Varois-
en-Provence
- Côtes de
Provence
- Palette
Rhône Valley
- Beaumes-de-
Venise, Muscat
de Beaumes-de-
Venise
- Cairanne
- Château-Grillet
- Châteauneuf-du-
Pape
- Clairette de Die
- Collines
Rhodaniennes
- Condrieu
- Cornas
- Costières de
Nîmes
- Coteaux de

l'Ardèche
- Côte-Rôtie
- Côtes du Rhône,
Côtes du Rhône-
Villages
- Côtes du Vivarais
- Crozes-
Hermitage
- Gigondas
- Hermitage
- Lirac
- Lubéron
- Rasteau
- St-Joseph
- St-Péray
- Tavel
- Vacqueyras
- Ventoux
- Vinsobres
Savoie
South-West
- Béarn
- Bergerac
- Buzet
- Cahors
- Coteaux de
Quercy
- Côtes de Duras
- Côtes de
Gascogne
- Côtes du
Marmandais
- Fronton
- Gaillac
- Irouléguy
- Jurançon
- Madiran

- Marcillac
- Monbazillac
- Montravel
- Pacherenc du
Vic-Bilh
- Pécharmant
- Rosette
- St-Mont
- Saussignac
- Tursan

GERMANY
Ahr
Baden
Franken
Hessische Bergstrasse
Mittelrhein
Mosel
Nahe
Pfalz
Rheingau
Rheinhessen
Saale-Unstrut
Sachsen
Württemberg

ITALY
Abruzzo
- Colline
Teramane
Alto Adige
Basilicata
- Aglianico del
Vulture
Calabria
- Cirò
Campania

- Taurasi

Emilia-Romagna
- Colli Piacentini

Friuli-Venezia Giulia
- Carso
- Colli Orientali del Friuli
- Collio
- Friuli Isonzo

Lazio
- Frascati

Liguria

Lombardy
- Franciacorta
- Lugana
- Oltrepò Pavese
- Valtellina Superiore

Marche
- Verdicchio dei Castelli di Jesi
- Verdicchio di Matelica
- Conero, Rosso Conero
- Rosso Piceno

Piedmont
- Asti, Moscato d'Asti
- Barbaresco
- Barbera d'Alba, d'Asti
- Barolo
- Dogliani
- Gattinara
- Gavi
- Langhe

- Nebbiolo d'Alba
- Roero

Puglia
- Primitivo di Manduria
- Castel del Monte
- Salice Salentino

Romagna

Sardinia
- Carignano del Sulcis

Sicily
- Etna
- Marsala
- Moscato Passito di Pantelleria

Trentino-Alto Adige
- Teroldego Rotaliano

Tuscany
- Bolgheri
- Brunello di Montalcino
- Carmignano
- Chianti, Chianti Classico, Chianti Rufina
- Morellino di Scansano
- Rosso di Montalcino
- Vernaccia di San Gimignano
- Vino Nobile di Montepulciano

Umbria
- Montefalco

- Orvieto

Valle d'Aosta

Veneto
- Amarone della Valpolicella
- Bardolino
- Bianco di Custoza
- Breganze
- Prosecco
- Soave, Recioto di Soave
- Valpolicella, Recioto della Valpolicella

NEW ZEALAND

Auckland
- Kumeu/Huapai
- Waiheke Island

Canterbury
- Waipara
- Waitaki

Central Otago
- Bannockburn

Gisborne

Hawkes Bay
- Gimblett Gravels

Marlborough
- Awatere

Nelson

Wairarapa
- Martinborough

PORTUGAL

Alentejo

Algarve

Azores
Bairrada
Beira Interior
Dão and Lafões
• Dão
Douro and Port
Lisboa
• Alenquer
• Bucelas
• Colares
Madeira
Península de Setúbal
• Palmela
• Setúbal
Távora-Varosa
Tejo
Trás-os-Montes
Vinho Verde
• *Minho*

SOUTH AFRICA
Breede River Valley
• Breedekloof
• Robertson
• Worcester
Cape South Coast
• Cape Agulhas
• Elgin
• Elim
• Hemel-en-Aarde
• Overberg
• Walker Bay
Coastal Region
• Constantia
• Durbanville
• Franschhoek
• Paarl

• Stellenbosch
• Swartland
• Wellington

SPAIN
Andalucía
• Jerez y
  Manzanilla
• Málaga
• Montilla-Moriles
Aragón
• Campo de Borja
• Calatayud
• Cariñena
• Somontano
Balearic Islands
Canary Islands
Castilla-La Mancha
• Jumilla
• La Mancha
• Manchuela
• Valdepeñas
Castilla y León
• Bierzo
• Ribera del
  Duero
• Rueda
• Toro
Cataluña
• Cava
• Costers del
  Segre
• Empordà
• Montsant
• Penedès
• Priorat
Extremadura

Galicia
• Rías Baixas
• Ribeiro
• Valdeorras
Madrid
• Manchuela
• Vinos de Madrid
Navarra
País Vasco
• Txakoli/Chacolí
Rioja
Valencia
• Utiel-Requena

SWITZERLAND
• Ticino
• Valais
• Vaud

USA
California
• Alexander Valley
• Anderson Valley
• Carneros
• Central Coast
• Chiles Valley
• Clarksburg
• Clear Lake
• Coombsville
• Diamond
  Mountain
  District
• Dry Creek
  Valley
• Howell
  Mountain
• Livermore

Valley
- Lodi
- Marin County
- Mount Veeder
- Napa Valley
- North Coast
- Oakville
- Paso Robles
- Russian River
  Valley
- Rutherford
- Santa Cruz
  Mountains
- Santa Maria
  Valley
- Santa Rita Hills
- Santa Ynez
  Valley
- Sierra Foothills
- Sonoma Coast,
  Sonoma Valley
- Spring
  Mountain
- Stags Leap
  District
- Yorkville
  Highlands

Colorado

Maryland

Michigan

New York State
- Finger Lakes
- Hudson River
- Long Island

Oregon
- Dundee Hills
- Eola-Amity Hills

- Willamette
  Valley

Pennsylvania

Texas
- Texas High
  Plains

Virginia
- Monticello
- Shenandoah
  Valley

Washington State
- Columbia Valley
- Red Mountain
- Walla Walla
  Valley
- Yakima Valley

WINE JARGON

These are the most common words that you may come across on a wine label or when visiting a producer.

A

AC/AOC/AOP (appellation d'origine contrôlée/protégée) The top category of French wines, defined by regulations covering vineyard yields, grape varieties, geographical boundaries, alcohol content and production method. Guarantees origin and style of a wine, but not its quality.

Acid/acidity Naturally present in grapes and essential to wine, providing balance and stability, a refreshing tang in white wines and appetizing grip in reds. Too much can make a wine taste sharp, too little and it will be flabby.

Aging May take place in vat, barrel or bottle, and may last for months or years. It has a mellowing effect on a wine, but if a wine is stored for too long it may lose its fruit.

Alcoholic content The alcoholic strength of wine, expressed as a percentage of the total volume of the wine. Typically in the range of 7–15%.

Alcoholic fermentation The process whereby yeasts, natural or added, convert the grape sugars into alcohol (ethyl alcohol, or ethanol) and carbon dioxide.

Amontillado Traditionally dry but rich style of aged sherry.

Auslese German and Austrian Prädikat category meaning that the grapes were 'selected' for their higher ripeness. The wines will often be sweet.

AVA (American Viticultural Area) System of appellations of origin for US wines.

Azienda agricola Italian for estate or farm. It also indicates wine made from grapes grown by the proprietor.

B

Barrel aging Time spent maturing in wood, usually oak, during which wine may take on flavours from the wood if new barrels are used.

Barrel fermentation Oak barrels may be used for fermentation instead of stainless steel to give a rich, oaky flavour to the wine.

Barrique The *barrique bordelaise* is the traditional Bordeaux oak barrel of 225 litres (50 gallons) capacity, used for aging and sometimes for fermenting wine. You will come across this term if you visit any winery anywhere in the world.

Beerenauslese German and Austrian Prädikat category applied to wines made from 'individually selected berries' (i.e. grapes), almost always affected by noble rot (*Edelfäule* in German). The wines are rich and sweet. Beerenauslese wines are only produced in the best years in Germany, but in Austria they are a regular occurrence.

Bin end Bin ends are simply leftovers, the last bottles of a particular vintage, and the retailer wants to clear them out to make room for the new vintage (or the retailer bought too much of a particular wine and wants to shift it). Either way, they may be offered at a reduced price. Often they are a bargain but there is always the risk that the wine may be past its best.

Biodynamic viticulture This approach works with the movement of the planets and cosmic forces to achieve health and balance in the soil and in the vine. Vines are treated with infusions of mineral, animal and plant materials, applied in homeopathic quantities. An increasing number of growers are turning to biodynamism, with some astonishing results, but it is labour-intensive and generally confined to smaller estates.

Blanc de blancs White wine made from one or more white grape varieties. Used especially for sparkling wines; in Champagne, denotes wine made entirely from the Chardonnay grape.

Blanc de noirs White wine made from black grapes only – the juice is separated from the skins to avoid extracting any colour. Most often seen in Champagne, where it describes wine made from Pinot Noir and/or Pinot Meunier grapes.

Blending The art of mixing together wines of different origin, style or age, often to balance out acidity, weight etc. Winemakers often use the term *assemblage*.

Bodega Spanish for winery.

Botrytis See noble rot.

Brut French term for dry sparkling wines, especially Champagne.

C

Carbonic maceration Winemaking method used to produce fresh fruity reds for drinking young. Whole (uncrushed) bunches of grapes are fermented in closed containers – a process that extracts lots of fruit and colour, but little tannin.

Champagne method Traditional method used for nearly all of the world's finest sparkling wines. A second fermentation takes place in the bottle, producing carbon dioxide which, kept in solution under pressure, gives the wine its fizz.

Chaptalization Legal addition of sugar during fermentation to raise a wine's alcoholic strength. More necessary in cool climates such as

Germany, where lack of sun may produce insufficient natural sugar in the grape. Also referred to as enrichment.

Château French for castle; widely used in France (and in some New World countries, too) to describe any wine estate, large or small.

Chiaretto Italian for a rosé wine of very light pink colour from around Lake Garda.

Claret English term for red Bordeaux wines, from the French *clairet*, which was traditionally used to describe a lighter style of red Bordeaux.

Clarification Term covering any winemaking process (such as filtering or fining) that involves the removal of solid matter either from the must or the wine.

Clos French for a walled vineyard – as in Burgundy's Clos de Vougeot – also commonly incorporated into the names of estates (e.g. Clos des Papes), whether they are walled or not.

Cold fermentation Long, slow fermentation at low temperature to extract maximum freshness from the grapes. Crucial for whites in hot climates.

Colheita Aged tawny port from a single vintage.

Commune A French village and its surrounding area or parish.

Co-operative In a co-operative cellar, growers who are members bring their grapes for vinification and bottling under a collective label. In terms of quantity, the French wine industry is dominated by co-ops. They often use less workaday titles, such as Caves des Vignerons, Producteurs Réunis, Union des Producteurs or Cellier des Vignerons.

Corked/corky Wine fault derived from a cork which has become contaminated, usually with Trichloroanisole or TCA. The mouldy, stale smell is unmistakable. Not pieces of cork in the wine.

Cosecha Spanish for vintage.

Côtes/coteaux French for slopes. Many, but not all, of the country's best vineyards are on hillside sites.

Crémant French term for traditional method sparkling wine from regions other than Champagne, for example Crémant de Limoux.

Crianza Spanish term for the process of aging a wine; also used as the youngest official category of matured wine. A red Crianza wine must be aged for at least 2 years (1 in oak, 1 in bottle) before sale, a white or rosé, 1 year.

Cru French for growth, meaning a specific plot of land or particular estate. In Burgundy, growths are divided into Grands (great) and Premiers (first) Crus, and apply solely to the actual land. In

Champagne the same terms are used for whole villages. In Bordeaux there are various hierarchical levels of Cru referring to estates rather than their vineyards. In Italy the term is used in an unofficial way, to indicate a single-vineyard or special-selection wine.

Cru classé The Classed Growths are the aristocracy of Bordeaux, ennobled by the Classifications of 1855 (for the Médoc, Barsac and Sauternes), 1955, 1969, 1986, 1996, 2006 and 2012 (for St-Émilion) and 1953 and 1959 (for Graves). Pomerol has never been classified. The modern classifications are more reliable than the 1855 version, which was based solely on the price of the wines at the time of the Great Exhibition in Paris, but in terms of prestige the 1855 Classification remains the most important. With the exception of a single alteration in 1973, when Ch. Mouton-Rothschild was elevated to First Growth status, the list has not changed since 1855. It certainly needs revising.

Cuve close Often known as the tank method, this bulk process used to produce inexpensive sparkling wines. The second fermentation, which produces the bubbles, takes place in tank rather than in the bottle (as in the superior traditional method). Also called Charmat.

Cuvée French for the contents of a single vat or tank, but usually indicates a wine blended from either different grape varieties or the best barrels of wine.

D

Dégorgement Stage of disgorgement in the production of Champagne-method wines when the sediment, collected in the neck of the bottle during *remuage* or riddling, is removed.

Demi-sec French for medium-dry.

DO/DOP/DOCa Spain's quality wine categories, regulating origin and production methods.

DOC/DOP Portugal's top quality wine classification.

DOP/DOC/DOCGg Italy's quality wine categories, regulating origin, grape varieties, yield and production methods.

Domaine French term for wine estate.

Dosage A sugar and wine mixture added to sparkling wine after *dégorgement* or disgorgement, which affects how sweet or dry it will be.

E

Eiswein Rare, chiefly German and Austrian, late-harvested wine made by picking the grapes and pressing them while frozen. This concentrates the sweetness of the grape as most of the liquid is removed as ice. See also Icewine.

Escolha Portuguese for selection.

Extraction Refers to the extraction of colour, tannins and flavour from the grapes during and after fermentation. There are various ways in which extraction can be manipulated by the winemaker, but over-extraction leads to imbalance.

F

Filtering Removal of yeasts, solids and any impurities from a wine before bottling.

Fining Method of clarifying wine by adding a coagulant (e.g. egg whites, isinglass) to remove soluble particles such as proteins and excessive tannins.

Fino The lightest, freshest style of sherry.

Flor A film of yeast which forms on the surface of fino sherries (and some other wines) in the barrel, preventing oxidation and imparting a tangy, dry flavour.

Fortified wine Wine that has high-alcohol grape spirit added, usually before the initial fermentation is completed, so preserving sweetness.

Frizzante Italian for semi-sparkling wine.

G

Gran reserva Top category of Spanish wines from a top vintage, with at least 5 years' aging (2 of them in cask) for reds and 4 for whites.

Grand cru French for 'great growth'. Supposedly the best vineyard sites in Alsace, Burgundy, Champagne and parts of Bordeaux (the Medoc, Graves, Sauternes and St-Émilion) – and should produce the most exciting wines.

H

Halbtrocken German for medium-dry.

I

Icewine A speciality of Canada, produced from juice squeezed from ripe grapes that have frozen on the vine. See also Eiswein.

IGP European classification of regional wines, replacing terms such as Vin de Pays in France, Vino da Tavola in Italy and other regional designations elsewhere. Both premium and everyday wines may share the same appellation.

K

Kabinett The least ripe level of QmP wines in Germany.

L

Landwein German or Austrian 'country' wine. The wine must have a territorial definition and may be chaptalized to give it more alcohol.
Late harvest Grapes are left on the vines beyond the normal harvest time to concentrate flavours and sugars. See also Vendange Tardive.
Laying down The storing of wine which will improve with age.
Lees Sediment – dead yeast cells, grape pips (seeds), pulp and tartrates – thrown by wine during fermentation and left behind after racking. Some wines are left on the fine lees for as long as possible to take on extra flavour. Look for the term *sur lie* on the label.

M

Maceration Important winemaking process for red wines whereby colour, flavour and/or tannin are extracted from grape skins before, during or after fermentation. The period lasts from a few days to several weeks.
Malolactic fermentation Secondary fermentation whereby harsh malic acid is converted into mild lactic acid and carbon dioxide. Normal in red wines but often prevented in whites to preserve a fresh, fruity taste.
Manzanilla The tangiest style of sherry, similar to fino.
Maturation Term for the beneficial aging of wine.
Meritage American term for red or white wines made from a blend of Bordeaux grape varieties.
Mesoclimate The climate of a specific geographical area, be it a vineyard or simply a hillside or valley.
Midi A loose geographical term, virtually synonymous with the large region of Languedoc-Roussillon, covering the vast, sunbaked area of southern France between the Pyrenees and the southern Rhône Valley.
Moelleux French for soft or mellow, used to describe sweet or medium-sweet wines, particularly in the Loire Valley (e.g. Saumur).
Mousseux French for sparkling wine.
Must Mixture of grape juice, skins, pips and pulp produced after crushing (prior to completion of fermentation), which will eventually become wine.

Must weight An indicator of the sugar content of juice – and therefore the ripeness of grapes.

'Natural' wines Movement originating in France and catching on in Italy, California and elsewhere as a counterpoint to the mass of 'industrial' wine. (Artisan) members seek to bring out the true expression of the soil 'naturally', i.e. by minimal intervention both in the vineyard and in the winery, notably without the addition of sulphur dioxide. This process is not yet regulated, resulting in a broad range of quality, from the exceptional to vinegar.

Négociant French term for a merchant who buys and sells wine. A *négociant-éléveur* is a merchant who buys, makes, ages and sells wine.

New World When used as a geographical term, New World includes the Americas, South Africa, Australia and New Zealand. And so, it is a term used to describe the fruity, upfront style of wine which is now in evidence all over the world, but pioneered in the USA and Australia.

Noble rot (*Botrytis cinerea*) Fungus which, when it attacks ripe white grapes, shrivels the fruit and intensifies their sugar while adding a distinctive flavour. A vital factor in creating many of the world's finest sweet wines, such as Sauternes and Trockenbeerenauslese.

O

Oak The wood most commonly used to make barrels for fermenting and aging fine wines. It adds flavours such as vanilla, and tannins; the newer the barrel, the greater the impact.

Oidium Fungal disease, also called powdery mildew, attacking vine leaves and shoots.

Oloroso The darkest, heaviest style of sherry, usually dry.

Orange wine A new style of wine from white grapes, popular with supporters of the 'natural' wine movement, that has ancient origins. The earliest winemakers would very likely have fermented their grapes whole – skins, pips and stalks all thrown in together. From white grapes, the resulting wine would have an orange colour and a rustic flavour. And that's the way some modern winemakers like it. Alternatively a white wine may be aged in clay amphoras before bottling, which also gives an 'orange' wine. Producers in Georgia prefer to call their claypot-fermented wines 'amber'. A subtler variation is the copper-coloured wine made from darker-skinned white grapes such as Pinot Gris, where the juice is left in contact with the skins for a short time before fermentation; this style is traditional to Friuli in north-east Italy, where it is known as *ramato*, meaning 'coppery'; some US producers now use this term.

Oxidation Over-exposure of wine to air, causing loss of fruit and flavour. Slight oxidation, such as occurs through the wood of a barrel or during racking, is part of the aging process and, in wines of sufficient structure, enhances flavour and complexity.

P

Passito Italian term for wine made from dried grapes. The result is usually a sweet wine with a raisiny intensity of fruit.

Perlwein German for a lightly sparkling wine.

Pétillant French for a lightly sparkling wine.

Phylloxera The vine aphid *Phylloxera vastatrix* attacks vine roots. It devastated vineyards around the world in the late 1800s soon after it arrived from America. Since then, the vulnerable *Vitis vinifera* has generally been grafted on to vinously inferior, but phylloxera-resistant, American rootstocks. Quality is supposedly unaffected.

Prädikat Grades defining quality wines in Germany and Austria. These are (in ascending order) Kabinett (not considered as Prädikat in Austria), Spätlese, Auslese, Beerenauslese, the Austrian-only category Ausbruch, and Trockenbeerenauslese. Strohwein and Eiswein are also Prädikat wines.

Premier cru First Growth: the top quality classification in parts of Bordeaux, but second to Grand Cru in Burgundy. Used in Champagne to designate vineyards just below Grand Cru.

Primeur French term for a young wine, often released for sale within a few weeks of the harvest. Beaujolais Nouveau is the best-known example. Bordeaux holds 'primeur' tastings in the April following the vintage.

Q

QbA (Qualitätswein bestimmter Anbaugebiete) German for quality wine from designated regions. Sugar can be added to increase the alcohol content. Often pretty ordinary, but from top estates this category offers excellent value and many hipster producers make use of it. In Austria Qualitätswein is equivalent to German QbA.

QmP (Qualitätswein mit Prädikat) See Prädikatswein.

Quinta Portuguese for farm or estate.

R

Racking Gradual clarification of wine: the wine is transferred from one barrel or container to another, leaving the lees behind.

Ramato See Orange wine.

Rancio Fortified wine deliberately exposed to the effects of oxidation, found mainly in Languedoc-Roussillon and parts of Spain.

Remuage Process in Champagne-making whereby the bottles, stored on their sides and at a progressively steeper angle in pupitres, are twisted, or riddled, each day so that the sediment moves down the sides and collects in the neck of the bottle on the cap, ready for *dégorgement* or disgorging. The English term is riddling.

Reserva Spanish wines that have fulfilled certain aging requirements: reds must have at least 3 years' aging before sale, of which one must be in oak barrels; whites and rosés must have at least 2 years' age, of which 6 months must be in oak.

Réserve French for what is, in theory, a winemaker's best wine. The word has no legal definition in France.

Ripasso A method used in Valpolicella to make wines with extra depth. Wine is passed over the lees of Recioto or Amarone della Valpolicella, adding extra alcohol and flavour, though also extra tannin and a risk of higher acidity and oxidation.

Riserva An Italian term for a special selection of wine that has been aged longer before release. It is only a promise of a more pleasurable drink if the wine had enough fruit and structure in the first place.

S

Saignée Rosé wine takes its colour from the skins of red grapes: the juice is bled off (*saignée*) after a short period of contact with the skins.

Sec French for dry. When applied to Champagne, it means medium-dry.

'Second' wines A second selection from a designated vineyard, usually lighter and quicker-maturing than the main wine (*grand vin*).

Sediment Usually refers to residue thrown by a wine, particularly red, as it ages in bottle.

Sekt German sparkling wine. The best wines are made by the traditional method, from 100% Riesling or 100% Weissburgunder (Pinot Blanc).

Sélection de grains nobles (SGN) A super-ripe category for sweet Alsace wines, now also being used by some producers of Coteaux du Layon in the Loire Valley.

Solera Spanish system of blending fortified wines, especially sherry and Montilla-Moriles. When mature wine is run off a cask for bottling, only a quarter or so of the volume is taken, and the cask is filled up with similar but younger wine taken from another cask, which in turn is topped up from an even younger cask, and so on.

Spätlese German for late-picked (riper) grapes. Often moderately sweet, though there are many dry versions.

Spumante Italian for sparkling. Bottle-fermented wines (as with Champagne) are often referred to as *metodo classico* or *metodo tradizionale*.

Supérieur French for a wine with a slightly higher alcohol content than the basic AC.

Superiore Italian DOC wines with higher alcohol or more aging potential.

Sur lie French for on the lees, meaning wine bottled direct from the cask/fermentation vat to gain extra flavour from the lees. Common with quality Muscadet, white Burgundy, similar barrel-aged whites and, increasingly, bulk whites.

T

Tannin Harsh, bitter, mouth-puckering element in red wine, derived from grape skins, pips and stems, and from oak barrels. Tannins soften with age and are essential for long-term development in red wines.

Terroir A French term used to denote the combination of soil, climate and exposure to the sun – that is, the natural physical environment of the vine.

Traditional method See Champagne method.

Trocken German for dry.

Trockenbeerenauslese (TBA) German for 'dry berry selected', denoting grapes affected by noble rot (*Edelfäule* in German) – the wines will be lusciously sweet although low in alcohol.

V

Varietal Wine made from, and named after, a single or dominant grape variety.

Velho Portuguese for old. Legally applied only to wines with at least 3 years' aging for reds and 2 years for whites.

Vendange tardive French for late harvest. The term is traditional in Alsace. The Italian term is *vendemmia tardiva*.

Vieilles vignes French term for a wine made from vines at least 20 years old. Most European countries have their own version. Should have greater concentration than wine from younger vines. Old vines is an imprecise but frequently used term in the New World.

Vin de garage Wines made on so small a scale they could be made in a garage. Such wines may be made from vineyards of a couple of hectares or less, and are often of extreme concentration.

Vin de paille Sweet wine found mainly in the Jura region of France. Traditionally, the grapes are left for two to three months on straw (*paille*) mats before fermentation to dehydrate, thus concentrating the sugars. The wines are sweet but slightly nutty and often have an attractive sour streak.

Vin doux naturel (VDN) French for a fortified wine, where fermentation has been stopped by the addition of alcohol, leaving the wine 'naturally' sweet, although you could argue that stopping fermentation with a slug of powerful spirit is distinctly unnatural.

Vin jaune A speciality of the Jura region in France, made from the Savagnin grape. Made in a similar way to fino sherry but not fortified, and aged for six years in oak. Unlike fino, *vin jaune* ages well.

Viña Spanish for vineyard.

Vinification The process of turning grapes into wine.

Vintage The year's grape harvest, also used to describe wines of a single year.

Viticulture Vine-growing and vineyard management.

Vitis vinifera Vine species, native to Europe and Central Asia, from which almost all the world's quality wine is made.

VQA (Vintners Quality Alliance) Canadian equivalent of France's AC system, defining quality standards and designated viticultural areas.

W

WO (Wine of Origin) South African system of appellations which certifies area of origin, grape variety and vintage.

Y

Yield The amount of fruit, and ultimately wine, produced from a vineyard. Measured in hectolitres per hectare (hl/ha) in most of Europe, and in the New World as tons per acre or tonnes per hectare. Yield may vary from year to year, and depends on grape variety, age and density of the vines, and viticultural practices.

Oz Clarke is one of the world's leading wine experts, known for his phenomenal palate, irreverent style, accurate predictions, and enthusiasm for life in general and wine in particular. He is the author of many award-winning books on wine. Before wine took over his life in 1984, Oz was a full-time actor and singer, appearing in West End hit shows and touring with the Royal Shakespeare Company. Alongside his entertaining BBC television and radio broadcasts, including 'Food and Drink' and 'Oz and James' with James May, he currently presents a series of concerts, Drink to Music! with the acclaimed Armonico Consort. Oz is also sports mad.